Henotes

Henotes

All Nations, United by Love

JENNIFER S. LEE

RESOURCE *Publications* • Eugene, Oregon

HENOTES
All Nations, United by Love

Copyright © 2024 Jennifer S. Lee. All rights reserved. Except for brief quotations in critical publications or reviews, no part of this book may be reproduced in any manner without prior written permission from the publisher. Write: Permissions, Wipf and Stock Publishers, 199 W. 8th Ave., Suite 3, Eugene, OR 97401.

Resource Publications
An Imprint of Wipf and Stock Publishers
199 W. 8th Ave., Suite 3
Eugene, OR 97401

Scripture quotations are taken from the Holy Bible, New International Version®, NIV® Copyright © 1973, 1978, 1984, 2011 by Biblica, Inc.™ Used by permission. All rights reserved worldwide.

www.wipfandstock.com

PAPERBACK ISBN: 979-8-3852-2806-5
HARDCOVER ISBN: 979-8-3852-2807-2
EBOOK ISBN: 979-8-3852-2808-9

VERSION NUMBER 100124

Contents

Chapter 1—**The Way** | 1
Chapter 2—**Our Offering** | 11
Chapter 3—**Personal Exodus** | 20
Chapter 4—**Commandments** | 32
Chapter 5—**United** | 42
Chapter 6—**The Veil of Soul** | 52
Chapter 7—**Holy Spirit** | 62
Chapter 8—**Easter** | 76
Chapter 9—**The Future** | 85
Chapter 10—**Angels** | 96
Chapter 11—**Prayer** | 107

Chapter 1

The Way

"A new command I give you: Love one another. As I have loved you, so you must love one another." (John 13:34)

The Christmas Snow

TODAY IS CHRISTMAS DAY, December 25th. On Christmas Day, everyone wishes for snow to have a White Christmas. According to information from the U.S. National White Christmas Map, it has been reported that for the past 130 years since 1893, there have been around 20 days, or approximately 16 percent, with measurable snow on the ground at Christmas day.

People around the world consider awaiting a White Christmas as a day to gather their long-missed family members in one place, sharing their lives and relieving their longing for each other. Rudolph pulls the sleigh with Santa; in every portrayal of these two characters, snow never fails to show their connectivity.

When I envision Christmas snow, it conjures memories of Rudolph, Santa, the heartfelt gifts exchanged, and the excitement for what's to come. Whether big or small, it doesn't matter; each moment is cherished, knowing they all stem from the love of my dearest family. Therefore, the snowfall during that time, even if it constitutes a small percentage, might become precious and special for creating a White Christmas.

However, there are extremely special things that we don't consider special at all, yet they are crucial elements in our lives. Sunlight, water, air, and, most importantly, the grace of God—these are gifts that no effort can purchased. The apostle Paul states in Galatians 5:19–21, "For it is by grace you have been saved, through faith—and this is not from yourselves, it is the gift of God—not by works, so that no one can boast." These are given freely to anyone, regardless of their worth or status, as an expression of God's love and character. God, whom we are unworthy of, desires to bridge the gap with us through grace, fostering a relationship of open communication.

How much do we truly understand the preciousness of grace? Our parents fed us, clothed us, and raised us from infancy to adulthood. There were times when we pleased them, moments when we might have annoyed or upset them. However, their love and upbringing were given freely.

Therefore, most of a parent's endless desire to provide what their children love, endlessly giving, stems from love and grace. There would hardly be any parent presenting a bill for all the years they've raised their children until adulthood. It's because, for over two decades, they've raised us not out of obligation but out of love and grace, simply because we are their children.

Let's consider another example: imagine an innocent person who, instead of me, bore the burden of my crime and spent twenty years in prison. I would live a life filled with gratitude for that person until my last breath. As I go about my days, if the thought of that person comes to mind, tears would involuntarily well up and, unknowingly, my head would bow in reverence. If that innocent person, who sought no repayment and served my sentence, asked for just an hour of conversation with me every week, would I refuse?

Now, imagine an innocent person who, seeking no recompense, went to the gallows in my place and died. How could one not be overwhelmed with tears of gratitude, feeling as though one's breath is taken away? In this world, there is no one else who would die in my stead; there's only one, and that is our Lord Jesus Christ. My Jesus, for me, endured being whipped, his flesh torn apart. A crown of thorns pierced his head because of my sins, causing blood to flow down his face. And for me a spear pierced his side, pouring out water and blood. Even a slight prick with a needle hurts, but for me they hammered nails into his hands and feet. It was for this sinner, for me, that God, as a proof of His love, selflessly gave His only Son, offering His life for us.

Who would give up their only beloved son to save someone insignificant like me? It's an unthinkable tale. However, this truth, an event incomprehensible to human understanding, is the grace bestowed upon us by an incomprehensible God. As stated in John 3:16–17, "For God so loved the world that he gave his one and only Son, that whoever believes in him shall not perish but have eternal life. For God did not send his Son into the world to condemn the world, but to save the world through him."
God saw us as invaluable treasures, not sparing even His own Son because of His love.

The Reason

God sent Jesus not to punish or condemn us but to save us through Him. He did so to give us an opportunity through Jesus and to save us in that manner. Can we truly feel the intense love God has for us, speaking about it because He ardently loves us? Until we resurrect as angels, we simply cannot measure that love. "When the dead rise,—they will be like the angels in heaven" (Mark 12:25).

At this point, a familiar question arises within me, one I've pondered before: why did God create humans in a way that salvation necessitates such a complex and arduous process from the start?

Typically, during the Christmas season, families gather to make various Christmas cookies such as chocolate toffee cookies, gingerbread cookies, sugar cookies, and cheesecake brownies to share together.

Imagining the joy of enjoying these treats with my family, I'm driven to make various desserts with my own determination. If a cookie doesn't turn out right or doesn't suit my taste, I discard it and start over, gathering ingredients until I achieve the desired beautiful cookies. Crafting these with care becomes an expression of my heart, and sprinkling the sparkle of Christmas decorations on the cookies brings happiness upon completion. The finished cookies don't question me about why I bothered to make them, despite the toil and time invested.

God, being the potter, can mold vessels as ordinary or as precious as He desires. The potter can instantly shatter them if desired, just as it is with God's heart and authority, as stated in Romans 9:21: "Does not the potter have the right to make out of the same lump of clay some pottery for special purposes and some for common use?"

The Scriptures often highlight a stark contrast between human tendencies and God's divine nature. While people tend to swiftly dismiss what they find unappealing or unfavorable, God, the very essence of grace and the epitome of love, exhibits a patient and enduring nature, slow to anger, and overflowing with unwavering love. Psalm 145:8 states, "The Lord is gracious and compassionate, slow to anger and rich in love."
This stark difference in response and behavior underscores the depth of God's compassion and patience compared to human impulses to quickly reject or discard. It's a profound reflection on the contrast of human flaws and divine grace.

The Forgiveness

From the first judgment after the sin of Adam and Eve to the second judgment upon all mankind—the flood during Noah's time—the progression of humanity's relationship with God underwent significant changes.

Adam, after being banished from Eden with Eve, had two sons, as we know: Cain and Abel. Cain, a tiller of the ground, offered some of the produce as an offering, while Abel brought the firstborn of his flock and their fat portions as an offering to God. God favored Abel's offering but did not favor Cain's. The exact reason for this in the Bible is not explicitly explained.

For what reason? Why did God accept Abel's offering but not Cain's?

As we continue reading the subsequent verses bring a speculative aspect. We might have clarification of the reason. Genesis 4:6 states, "Then the Lord said to Cain, 'Why are you angry? Why is your face downcast? If you do what is right, will you not be accepted? But if you do not do what is right, sin is crouching at your door; it desires to have you, but you must rule over it.'"
It is inferred that Cain offered his sacrifice with a heart that God considered not right, as Cain's countenance fell in anger because God did not favor his offering.

Enraged, Cain lured Abel into the field and attacked him, resulting in his death. When God, presumably aware of the truth, asked Cain where his brother was, Cain responded arrogantly, without guilt or shame: "Then the Lord said to Cain, 'Where is your brother Abel?' 'I don't know,' he replied. 'Am I my brother's keeper?'" (Genesis 4:9). Listen to Cain! How dare he talk back to God with a such an attitude!

The first recorded instance of murder in Human history was met with Cain's bad attitude toward God. Could someone who had just killed his brother dare to confront God in this manner? Does this seem like a response borne of a conscience?

If I, as a human, had enragedly killed someone, especially my own sibling, I would be headed to prison. The entire TV and internet would label me as a devil. I would face condemnation from my parents, siblings, friends, and acquaintances. Every relationship I had in the world would be shattered, and no one would acknowledge me solely because I would be a sinner.

So, God cursed Cain and drove him away from the land. Then, seemingly without feeling any remorse,

> Cain said to the Lord, "My punishment is more than I can bear. Today you are driving me from the land, and I will be hidden from your presence; I will be a restless

> wanderer on the earth, and whoever finds me will kill me." But the Lord said to him, "Not so, anyone who kills Cain will suffer vengeance seven times over." Then the Lord put a mark on Cain so that no one who found him would kill him. So, Cain went out from the Lord's presence and lived in the land of Nod, east of Eden. (Genessis 4:13–16)

Examining the conversation between God and Cain sheds lighter on why God did not accept Cain's offering. It's attributed to Cain's attitude from a vicious, evil heart—his lack of remorse for killing his brother Abel. Cain only cared about himself, showing no remorse for his brother Abel's death. He was entirely self-centered, displaying no concern for the anguish his parents or God might endure because of Abel's suffering. It demonstrates sheer selfishness and a lack of concern.

He was only about how he couldn't bear the punishment he received, not admitting to the crime, not expressing repentance, nor seeking forgiveness. It's not about acknowledging the gravity of the murder but about finding it unbearable to face the difficult punishment from God.

Cain, undeserving of God's grace and love, resents the God who did not accept his offering, kills Abel, and assumes nobody will ever find out. Nevertheless, God, to protect Cain, gave him some kind of mark.

What is God like? God is patient and compassionate, a God of grace and love.

The Purpose and Plan

After the incident with Cain, "The LORD saw how great the wickedness of the human race had become on the earth, and that every inclination of the thoughts of the human heart was only evil all the time. The LORD regretted that he had made human beings on the earth, and his heart was deeply troubled" (Genesis 6:5–6).

This illustrates that God deeply regretted creating humans, reflecting profound sadness because of how the wickedness of humanity had spread across the world, and God, observing people's thoughts and intentions always leaning toward evil, lamented this state of affairs. God's patience had reached its limit, He being unable to fulfill His purpose and plan for creating humankind. Therefore, God chose Noah, a righteous man, to carry out the plan of constructing an ark.

According to the information presented in the Bible, from the creation of Adam to Noah's flood, the total span of time is estimated to be around 1,656 years. I can't fathom God's patience enduring for over 1,600 years toward humanity. I might not have lasted a year without losing my temper, maybe even pulling out all my hair in frustration.

The rampant wickedness at that time is described in Genesis 6:2: "The sons of God saw that the daughters of humans were beautiful, and they married any of them they chose. Then the LORD said, 'My Spirit will not contend with humans forever, for they are mortal; their days will be a hundred and twenty years.'"
It's mentioned that the sons of God saw that the daughters of humans were beautiful and took any they chose as wives. God also declared that His Spirit would not remain with humans forever.

Who are the "sons of God"? "My Spirit will not contend with humans forever"? This verse is quite challenging to interpret. Some interpret this verse as indicating a separation between the spiritual and human realms. The statement about their days being 120 years may not be an indication of eternity.

Some scholars reference Matthew 22:30, where Jesus states that the angels in heaven do not marry. However, certain Christian writers interpret the "sons of God" in Genesis 6:4 ("The Nephilim were on the earth in those days—and also afterward—when the sons of God went to the daughters of humans and had children by them. They were the heroes of old, men of renown.") as referring to fallen angels who illicitly engaged with human women, resulting in the birth of the Nephilim. This interpretation suggests that the "sons of God" were not human.

Who or what exactly were the Nephilim? My research suggests they were enigmatic figures, often regarded as the "sons of

God"—fallen angels who fathered the Nephilim through unions with human women. This perspective is detailed in the book of First Enoch, considered noncanonical yet widely accepted. According to biblical genealogy, Enoch was Noah's great-grandfather. Enoch was the father of Methuselah, who, in turn, was the father of Lamech, who was Noah's father, and Enoch was in the Bible.

It's mentioned that Enoch did not experience death like most humans. Instead, it is said that God "took" Enoch directly to heaven. Genesis 5:24 describes that "Enoch walked faithfully with God; then he was no more, because God took him away."

Then a perplexing question arises in my mind: if Enoch the faithful righteous man wrote the book, by what discerning criteria was the book of First Enoch consigned to the category of noncanonical texts? And who, among scholars or religious figures, wielded the authority to render such a significant decision?

Additionally, Moses recorded the five books of the Pentateuch: Genesis, Exodus, Leviticus, Numbers, and Deuteronomy. He was raised in the Egyptian court and educated as a scholar, statesman, and military leader. He is regarded as a religious leader according to worldly perceptions. He transcribed these five books in the vicinity of Mount Sinai and the wilderness. The events chronicled in these books took place between approximately 4004 BC and 1689 BC.

The Nephilim are referenced in Numbers 13:33: "We saw the Nephilim there (the descendants of Anak come from the Nephilim). We seemed like grasshoppers in our own eyes, and we looked the same to them." This verse suggests the existence of giants in those times. It's said that during that time there were giants on the earth, offspring from the "sons of God" who entered the daughters of humans and bore children, mighty men of old, famous warriors.

Punishment or Salvation

God observed that human hearts and thoughts were filled with sin and regretted creating such corrupt beings on the earth. To purge the wicked from the land, God, in companionship with Noah, a righteous man who found grace in God's eyes, chose to execute a massive flood.

Returning to the recent discussion: if God forgave the transgression of Adam and Eve and later pardoned the heinous crime of Cain, protecting and sparing him, enduring for over a millennium, why then did God have to eradicate humans from the earth with Noah's flood?

God's plan involved creating this world, fashioning man and woman, and bestowing blessings upon them. As stated in Genesis 1:27: "God blessed them and said to them, 'Be fruitful and increase in number; fill the earth and subdue it. Rule over the fish in the sea and the birds in the sky and over every living creature that moves on the ground.'"

Genesis doesn't just talk about human transgressions; the distinctive aspect is the involvement of not humans but "sons of God," corrupting the lineage of humanity created by God.

In my brief view, I interpret this event as an act stemming from God's love, grace, and mercy to preserve the humans created in His holy image. God used Noah's family and pairs of animals to rebuild the human lineage, cleansing it from corruption.

Through numerous readings of the Bible and the profound experience of God's unwavering love in my life, I've come to a humble conclusion: In His infinite patience, God refrained from immediate destruction, patiently waiting for over a thousand years, hoping for a transformative shift in human behavior. However, meticulously considering every option, He ultimately chose the flood as a measure to reset humanity. It was a decisive step to restore the purity, cleanliness, and multifaceted nature of humanity, aligning with God's original intent.

And God established the rainbow as a covenant, promising to never again bring destruction upon humanity through water as stated in Genesis 9:12–15:

> And God said, "This is the sign of the covenant I am making between me and you and every living creature with you, a covenant for all generations to come: I have set my rainbow in the clouds, and it will be the sign of the

covenant between me and the earth. Whenever I bring clouds over the earth and the rainbow appears in the clouds, I will remember my covenant between me and you and all living creatures of every kind. Never again will the waters become a flood to destroy all life."

Another remarkable event unfolded two thousand years ago, on the same day as Christmas Day. Through God's love and grace, in the land of Judea, in Bethlehem, God sent His only begotten Son to us. In a poignant twist of fate, Jesus was born in the humblest of settings: a lowly manger, a crude and smelly hut. There were no lavish accommodations reserved for His arrival, no ornate chambers adorned in anticipation of His birth. Instead, He graced this world amidst the earthy scent of hay and the gentle lowing of livestock, surrounded by the rustic simplicity of a manger. He was born in the lowest and humblest place on earth to save us, the humble ones—for me.

His name is Jesus. What a great name, amazing name, powerful name that is!

For us, for me, God sent Himself out of love for us, to save us, and to grant eternal salvation if we accept Jesus as our Savior. I am so grateful for God's love and grace. I just want to speak of the name of Jesus on Christmas, on his birthday. I can't stop speaking about Jesus. I want to continue to speak of Jesus. This is an ongoing story.

Chapter 2

Our Offering

PB Diet

I, AS A CHRISTIAN, do not celebrate Halloween, but during that period I take benefit of the huge sales. I usually buy discounted candies like Reese's Peanut Butter Cups, M&M's, Skittles, and other candies small chocolate wrappers at up to 50 percent off. I bring them to the office and share them with colleagues every year. In one year, I purchased candies as much as I wanted, and upon checking the receipt, it showed a total of $50. However, since I bought them at a 50 percent discount, the result indicates that I bought $100 worth of candies.

I thought I bought a bit too much candy, but with a happy smile due to the 50 percent discount, I took them to work and enjoyed them with my colleagues. After a month or so, one day, I looked at a colleague who had been working in front of me for over ten years. Suddenly, I couldn't remember their name, so I glanced at the face of the colleague next to them. Again, I couldn't recall the name of that colleague either, whom I face every day. My heart sank, and It feeling like it dropped to the ground. I started to fearfully wonder if maybe a mild form of dementia was creeping in even at my young age.

At times while standing and working, I'd been experiencing symptoms of palpitations in my heart. It wouldn't stop, so I would crouch down and sit on the floor for a few seconds, waiting for my heartbeat to return to normal. The symptoms of mild amnesia and palpitations had been ongoing for a few months, and though it started to worry me a bit, I thought it might get better with time without needing to consult a doctor.

One Saturday afternoon, I watched a documentary program on TV and I found it very intriguing and moving. The documentary explained how limiting animal-based and processed foods and instead consuming a whole-plant diet, including whole grains, beans, vegetables, and fruits, can improve chronic illnesses. It detailed the careers of American cardiologist Caldwell Esselstyn and nutritional biochemistry professor T. Colin Campbell, discussing how they've treated many diseases including obesity, cardiovascular diseases, and cancer.

Dr. Esselstyn conducted an experiment with about ten or so patients with stage 4 cancer, all of whom had given up on treatment and were just waiting to die. Except for a few who dropped out of the experiment, all the patients are still healthy and alive, defying the odds and providing testimonials in interviews.

The daily consumption of a plant-based diet, avoiding processed foods and dairy and animal products, was said to be a preventative and therapeutic measure. Professor Campbell published *The China Study*,[1] a book based on his twenty-year research project in China, stating that heart disease, diabetes, obesity, and cancer could be linked to the Western diet, including processed and dairy-based animal foods in the SAD (Standard American Diet).

Fountain of Youth

The plant-based diet comprises entirely plant-based foods, emphasizing a variety of dietary patterns that limit or restrict animal

---

1. T. Colin Campbell and Thomas M. Campbell, *The China Study: The Most Comprehensive Study of Nutrition Ever Conducted and the Startling Implications for Diet, Weight Loss and Long-Term Health* (Dallas: Benbella, 2004).

products while incorporating high quantities of plant foods such as vegetables, fruits, whole grains, legumes, nuts, and seeds. This diet also avoids another set of highly processed, white foods: white sugar, white salt, white flour, and white rice. These have very limited nutritional value.

It also restricts the intake of fats and oils that rapidly absorb energy without undergoing proper digestion in the body. Fish and shellfish like shrimp, crab, and lobster, clams, scallops, and oysters etc. are not recommended due to their high concentration of mercury. However, some vitamins are only found in animal foods and can be harder to find in a plant-based diet. They are vitamins B12 and D, for which it is recommended to take supplements.

Moreover, it is recommended to consume only small amounts of vegetable or fruit juice due to their high concentration of nutrients, which could have a big impact on the liver when absorbed quickly, potentially leading to adverse effects. Instead, it suggested to chew fresh vegetables or fruits thoroughly to allow the enzymes present in saliva to aid in slow and proper digestion and absorption.

The abundance of processed foods today, rather than meats, is both a blessing and a curse. On one hand, avoiding animal products has become easier, with many of our consumables being offered as plant-based or vegan alternatives. However, giving up the aroma and taste of bacon, eggs, hamburgers, milk, and cheese, even with restricted animal-product intake, remains quite challenging. Yet, there are delightful vegan products available that tackle this issue, produced through elaborate manufacturing processes.

Some hardships experienced by individuals on a plant-based or vegan diet involve the processed vegan dairy and meat substitutes, which often contain high levels of salt, sugar, and fats. Additionally, they might include pesticides, unwanted additives, and preservatives. Therefore, I prefer purchasing as many organic items as possible.

Observing my symptoms, I decided to try the plant-based diet, thinking about my heart condition. There were no restrictions on portion sizes, and planning meals, buying ingredients, and adjusting to this diet was quite simple. It's been over five years since I started, and I am incredibly satisfied and will continue this path. A month after starting, my body began to change; I started emitting a pleasant body odor, and I lost thirty-five pounds by following a plant-based diet, without exercising, within the guidelines.

Dr. Esselstyn explained that our blood vessels are structured in three layers: the inner layer, middle layer, and outer layer. He described how even when our bodies digest animal-based foods in very small particles, they collide with the blood vessel walls, causing damage and leading to the accumulation of fats and cholesterol.

He likened this to the phenomenon of when a scratch occurs on a table or plastic surface, and gradually accumulates dirt. Therefore, he mentioned that it takes about three years on a plant-based diet for the inner lining of our blood vessels to regenerate. He suggested that as our blood vessels become healthier through this dietary approach, we would experience a fountain of youth alongside healing.

That statement is indeed true, and an unexpected bonus—not turning into a baby like the movie *The Curious Case of Benjamin Button*, but experiencing a reversal of about ten years in aging. I tracked the progress of my diet by taking before-and-after pictures every month. However, I stopped taking pictures two years after I've started my diet because my weight had stabilized close to my high school weight.

For transparency, I affirm that I have not received any endorsements from doctors or companies in relation to the plant-based diet presented in this book. The information provided is solely based on my personal experience.

Does God Love Fat?

In the plant-based diet, fats and oils are also restricted, which are consumed in very minimal amounts as needed. This reminds me of a Bible verse where God mentions the fat being His own: "The priest shall burn them on the altar as a food offering, a pleasing aroma. All the fat is the Lord's." (Leviticus 3:16). The passage explicitly states that "all the fat is the Lord's." Even with a plant-based diet, consuming a small amount of fat or oil is inevitable. For instance, even the lowest-fat-content hamburger patty still contains 2 percent fat. Leviticus 7:22–25 states:

> The Lord spoke to Moses, saying, "Speak to the people of Israel, saying, you shall eat no fat, of ox or sheep or goat. The fat of an animal that dies of itself and the fat of one that is torn by beasts may be put to some other use, but on no account shall you eat it. For every person who eats of the fat of an animal of which a food offering may be made to the Lord shall be cut off from his people."

Have you ever wondered why God loves fat? No matter how much we think or strive, it seems impossible to avoid fat intake completely. Being cut off from one's people for eating fat? Isn't that a very frightening statement? What could all this mean?

Biologically, the body stores energy temporarily for survival when needed. In essence, storing excess fat is a temporary provision for the future, to be utilized when required. When the food we eat gets converted into energy, the body stores what is more than necessary as fat. Then when we continue to add on top of what is already stored in our body and more, we label it as "obesity."

Leviticus 3:9 states, "Then he shall offer from the sacrifice of the peace offering, as an offering made by fire to the Lord, its fat and the whole fat and the whole fat tail which he shall remove close to the backbone. And the fat that covers the entrails and all the fat that is on the entrails." When offering a peace offering of a lamb, it's recorded to present "the fat tail" to God. Among theologians, this part is interpreted as the most precious.

In Leviticus, when presenting a peace offering to God, the specific instruction to offer the oil or fat as a burnt offering is laden with profound significance. It serves as a tangible expression of reverence and devotion, highlighting the importance of offering the choicest portions as a symbol of utmost respect for the Divine. This command resonates with the idea of sacrificial giving, emphasizing the notion of giving generously and selflessly to honor God.

The Burned Offering and Fellowship Offering

According to biblical scholars, the burnt offering was for receiving forgiveness of sins, while the fellowship offering aimed for forgiveness. The purpose of the fellowship offering was to share intimate communion with God. It's also called the "sacrifice of peace," as stated in Leviticus 3:3–5:

> From the fellowship offering, he is to bring a food offering to the Lord: the fat that covers the internal organs and all the fat that is connected to them, both kidneys with the fat on them near the loins, and the long lobe of the liver, which he will remove with the kidneys. The priest shall burn them on the altar as a food offering, a pleasing aroma. All the fat is the Lord's.

When humans sinned, we were in enmity with God. However, through the ministry of Jesus Christ's cross, we can now have fellowship with God in peace. The burnt offering involves burning everything except the animal's skin on the altar. Since the offering symbolized the animal dying in place of my sin, it had to be completely burnt to ashes.

Are we genuinely presenting God with our very best? When the Israelites offered the fellowship offering, including oil in the offering signified presenting something of utmost preciousness and value. Our most treasured offerings are not merely material possessions but are crafted from the depths of our being—our inner core, the hearts and mind, which in turn guide our actions. Pure thought is the vehicle to create cleanness of life.

Moreover, those who offered the fellowship sacrifice presented the kidneys. The kidneys are where a person's deep emotions, thoughts, and conscience were thought to reside. Also, offering the liver carried a similar significance, as it is one of the heaviest organs. The liver, symbolizing profound human emotions, mirrors both immense joy and deep sorrow.

While the consumption of chopped liver might not suit everyone's taste, the English saying "What am I, chopped liver?" signifies frustration or anger resulting from feeling ignored socially. It's as if someone's entire sense of joy is broken into fragmented pieces, turning delight into despair. Therefore, offering the kidneys and liver to God during the fellowship sacrifice symbolized offering our hearts, our core, to God.

When we worship God, our bodies may be in the church, but our hearts may be elsewhere, preoccupied with worldly thoughts, worries, and human plans. However, just as offering the kidneys and liver during the fellowship sacrifice holds meaning, when we gather to worship together, offering our hearts to God is essential, as stated in Jeremiah 11:20: "But you, Lord Almighty, who judge righteously and test the heart and mind, let me see your vengeance on them, for to you I have committed my cause."

If we don't offer our hearts to God during worship, it holds no meaning. Above all, God desires our hearts, our core, that most important part we can offer to our God, to our Creator.

Sharing Joy and Delight

Most importantly, when offering the fellowship sacrifice, one can present a bull, a lamb, or a goat. The "fat," the best parts—liver, kidneys—are offered to God. The breast portion and the right rear leg are given to the priest who conducts the sacrifice, and the rest belongs to the person making the offering. However, let's focus on one crucial aspect here.

Leviticus 7:15 states, "The meat of their fellowship offering of thanksgiving must be eaten on the day it is offered; they must leave none of it till morning." What happens if the person offering the fellowship sacrifice doesn't consume all of it? It's stated that the fellowship offering becomes abominable. The sacrifice isn't accepted by God, and the dedicated individual incurs guilt before God.

Therefore, the one offering the sacrifice must consume everything within the designated time frame.

Now, let's imagine for a moment: what animals are used for the fellowship offering? A bull, sheep, and goats. For instance, let's consider offering one bull as a fellowship sacrifice. The internal organs like fat, kidneys, and liver are dedicated to God, and thereafter the breast portion and the right rear leg are given to the priest conducting the fellowship sacrifice. However, how substantial is one bull? When one slaughters an average-sized bull, it could sufficiently feed numerous people.

If the meat from this significant bull isn't fully consumed by the next day, the fellowship sacrifice becomes invalid, not accepted by God. But could the person who offered the sacrifice consume it all in a day or the next day? What should they do?

They must invite family, relatives, friends, and neighbors to share and eat together. Therefore, the fellowship sacrifice always culminates in a communal meal, concluding the sacrifice by sharing it together. The essence of the fellowship sacrifice lies not only in the offered but also in the joy and grace experienced by those around the offering.

The fellowship offering truly demonstrates the form of worship desired by God. Faith isn't merely about believing in God and finding joy alone; it's about sharing the joy and peace that I experience with my neighbors, as illustrated in Psalm 133:1–3:

> How good and pleasant it is when God's people live together in unity! It is like precious oil poured on the head, running down on the beard, running down on Aaron's beard, down on the collar of his robe. It is as if the dew of Hermon were falling on Mount Zion. For there the LORD bestows his blessing, even life forevermore.

Worshipping alone in the church, solely focused on personal belief and benefit, falls short of the worship desired by God. True worship initiates with a heartfelt communion with God, but it doesn't end there. It extends to sharing the joy and blessings bestowed by God with our brothers and sisters in Christ. This interconnectedness reflects the essence of love within the Christian

Our Offering

community, where the bonds of brotherhood and sisterhood are strengthened through mutual support and sharing in the joy of worship that God truly desires from us as his children.

For our worship to genuinely please God, we must offer the most precious to the Lord. We should offer not only our bodies but also our hearts to the Lord. Because God desires our core above all else, it's about sharing the joy and delight granted by the Lord with our brothers and sisters around us.

It's all about worshipping God in harmony together in the church. We gather in the embrace of the church, our hearts tuned to the harmony of worship, lifting our voices in unison to honor God. Together, our souls intertwine, weaving a spiritual connection that strengthens and uplifts us. As the melodies of praise fill the air, our spirits are deepening our faith and enriching our souls.

After the service concludes, we remain united, continuing our fellowship in the warmth of shared company. Gathering outside the church walls, we convene for intimate connection in small Bible studies, where we delve into the sacred texts, seeking guidance and wisdom to navigate life's journey. In prayer circles, we offer supplication for one another, celebrating joys and offering peace in times of hardship. Each moment spent in communion with our fellow believers draws us closer to God, enriching our Christian lives with love, support, and unwavering faith.

During Bible study sessions, we approach the text with reverence and humility, recognizing that each passage holds layers of meaning waiting to be revealed to and recognized by us. We listen attentively to each other's interpretations, respecting diverse perspectives while seeking common ground in our shared faith.

In moments of prayer, thee air is filled with the earnest petitions of believers lifting their worries, sorrows, pains, concerns, joys, happiness, and victories to God. And we ask for His guidance and courage. We stand together in solidarity as standing on the rock, interceding on behalf of those in need and rejoicing in answered prayers. And as we bow our heads in reverence, we feel the presence of the Divine drawing us closer together, knitting our hearts together in God's grace and mercy.

Chapter 3

Personal Exodus

A Legend

I WANT TO INTRODUCE a female legend. She was born a few years after the Korean War, during political turmoil and poor economic conditions. The Korean War lasted only three years, but its effects were devastating. North and South Korea combined lost about 5.2 million lives, and the civilian casualties were much higher than in other wars. In addition, a huge number of families were separated, about ten million.

After the war, the economies of North and South Korea were in ruins. Almost all infrastructure, including schools, hospitals, factories, and roads, was destroyed. Mining and industrial and agricultural production declined by at least 60 percent and as much as 80 percent, and the number of Koreans displaced from their homes reached nearly two million. Between 20 and 25 percent of the population of the Korean peninsula faced a hunger crisis, and property damage was equivalent to the 1949 gross national product, resulting in a 14 percent drop in gross domestic product.

This female legend was eight years old when her family was displaced by the war, and they were forced to set up huts in the mountains and roam the streets and hillsides in search of food.

Personal Exodus

She ate wild plants in the mountains, dug up tree roots to make porridge with rice, and found old canned food in the streets and trash cans that soldiers had abandoned.

A younger brother was born, but due to her mother's malnutrition, his long limbs were weak and he looked a like a worry doll without colorful wool on it. He could not carry his own weight and could not speak. Though still breastfed by his mother, he died of starvation before reaching the age of two. The next year her mother had another baby boy, but this one didn't make it past the age of one and also died of starvation.

The economy gradually recovered, and the daughter matured into a twenty-year-old woman who had lost her two younger siblings. She had an older brother who had survived to join the army, a service that every Korean man of age must performed once for their military duty. She cherished her only brother and always worried about him, so she decided to visit him.

On the day she went to visit her brother at the frontline of DMG, he was excited to hear that his sister was coming to visit, so he quickly packed up his things and rushed to the visiting room, where his sister and about ten military police guards stood against the wall around the ark to keep an eye on the visitors. As he arrived, he could see his sister's face, beaming with joy, waiting for him.

As he hurried toward the table where she was seated, two military policemen blocked his path and told him to step aside as they needed to inspect his belongings. As the military police inspected his uniform from top to bottom, it was revealed to them that, in the excitement of meeting his sister, he had forgotten to put his gun and ammunition in storage and had accidentally worn it around his waist to the visiting room. Upon discovering this, the military police began to beat him viciously for disregarding military regulations. His nose began to bleed, but the military police kept kicking him with their hard army boots, and the beating continued unabated.

She ran to the military police and dragged her knees to the ground, crying and begging them to forgive him just this once. The military police forcefully pushed her to get out of their way and the beating continued. She felt so bad that she kept begging them with tears that she would do anything they wanted to save her brother and forgive him for his mistake.

When the military police heard this, he turned and looked at his fellows, stopped beating her brother, and asked her if she was sure she wanted to do whatever they wanted. With that, he led her out of the interview room and told her that he would forgive her brother if she lied down with him.

She agreed to his terms, willing to do anything to save her brother from the horrific violence, and a short time later he took her to his quarters. She gritted her teeth and closed her eyes to endure the humiliation, and when she tried to get up after the horrible act, she says she only remembers seeing more than ten military police started to come in the room, one after another, and one by one they removed their waistbelt. After the incident, she says, her brother became an alcoholic out of guilt and lived the rest of his life with it.

A few years past, one day, she went to watch a concert band made and played by US soldiers as a hobby, and she met and eventually married her ex-husband, who played guitar in the band. During their eleven-year marriage, he had Othello syndrome and would beat her when he was angry, inflicting mental and physical pain.

They had two children, a daughter and a son. Her daughter was diagnosed with leukemia at the age of twenty-one and died after a five-year battle. About a year after her death, her son ran away to Canada, leaving a note for her saying he was gay and didn't think she would accept him. He was the only child she had left, so she convinced him to move back in.

One day, she heard an American pastor preach on TV and, very moved by that, decided to go to church and started attending. Due to her husband's Othello syndrome, he beat her unspeakably for going to church because he thought she was having an affair with a man. And then he beat her again, and repeatedly. When her husband's physical abuse happened, and she was covered with bruises and battered, she escaped to any church that had their doors open to the public. Despite the beatings and persecution, she continued to go to church, which led to her husband divorcing her.

I can't fathom how anyone could endure such dreadful events for so many years, even decades. It's painful, almost unbelievable, because it weaves together an intricate pattern of unthinkable occurrences.

By the grace of God, she has begun her personal exodus. Her name is Young E. I am eternally grateful to her for sharing her testimony with me and freely allowing me to use it in my book.

Here's what we know about Othello syndrome. "The name Othello syndrome comes from the play Othello by William Shakespeare. It's similar to the way people who suffer from pathological jealousy fabricate evidence to prove an affair. Also, like Othello in the play, they are highly suspicious of infidelity, and this is done with obsession. One of the psychoses involved is visual hallucinations. Othello syndrome is a type of paranoid delusional jealousy. People who suffer from pathological jealousy may use physical and mental violence against their partners.

On several visits to my former aunt's house, I saw that the husband of the couple who rented the downstairs apartment suffered from this syndrome, and he was often violent toward his wife, and she took refuge in my aunt's house to escape it.

Above all, Young E. lived for decades with a lot of hurt, pain, and suffering from her family, society, and her husband, until she made a personal exodus to the land of honey and milk, the church, through a modern-day Moses, a pastor who appeared on TV.

What is your legend? What is your exodus?

Another Legend

Next up, we have a male legend. His name is Moses, and he led the Israelites out of slavery in Egypt in the book of Exodus. The biblical books of Genesis, Exodus, Leviticus, Numbers, and Deuteronomy were written by Moses and are called the Five Books of Moses, and this is one of them. Biblical scholars say they were written around 1446–1450 BC.

Significant evidence that Moses wrote them is found in Luke 24:44: "He said to them, "This is what I told you while I was still with you: Everything must be fulfilled that is written about me in the Law of Moses, the Prophets and the Psalms." Here Jesus himself refers to the Law of Moses, but the final author is God, and it was written by inspiration.

The book of Exodus can be seen as the fulfillment of the covenant to multiply him when God stopped by Abraham's tent before going to spy on Sodom and Gomorrah, telling Abraham that Sarah would give birth to a son.

> "Abraham will surely become a great and powerful nation, and all nations on earth will be blessed through him. For I have chosen him, so that he will direct his children and his household after him to keep the way of the Lord by doing what is right and just, so that the Lord will bring about for Abraham what he has promised him." (Genesis 18:18)

> "Then the Lord said to him, 'Know for certain that for four hundred years your descendants will be strangers in a country not their own and that they will be enslaved and mistreated there. But I will punish the nation they serve as slaves, and afterward they will come out with great possessions.'" (Genesis 15:13–14)

God fulfills his promise to Abraham that his descendants would suffer in foreign lands for four hundred years before returning to the promised land of Canaan.

Short Exodus Story

We will look at the book of Exodus as a summary and as a short story. Jacob and Joseph brought about seventy of their kin to Goshen in Egypt, and by the grace of God their kin multiplied and filled the earth. As the Israelites prospered, the Egyptian king harassed them and burdened them with building the treasury's castles.

And the more Pharaoh abused the Israelites, the more they flourished, so he continued to harass them, forcing them to bake bricks and do farm work. When the Israelites continued to thrive, the Pharaoh commanded Hebrew midwives to eliminate newborn Hebrew boys.

These brave women of God, the midwives, defied the king's order and kept the boys alive, and God was so impressed with their faith that he favored them and let them live well and prospers. You can see that when we believe in our God, we are bold in our faith and fearless. King Pharaoh's order to kill all male babies by throwing them into the Nile was a great rebellion against God, as it would have exterminated a people.

Moses was born to the tribe of Levi, and his mother hid him for three months before she was forced to put him in a basket and float him down the Nile. Moses was noticed by Pharaoh's daughter and raised as her adopted son, educated as if having royal blood. The name Moses means "to deliver," and he would become the deliverer of the Israelites. Moses was raised by the daughter of Pharaoh but his biological mother, Jochebed, came in as a nanny for two years. This shows God's protection to his beloved children, as stated in Luke 10:19: "I have given you power to trample on serpents and scorpions and to break all the power of your enemies, and now no mam will hurt you."

As we read this great story, one Bible verse came to me: "In their heart's humans plan their course, but the Lord establishes their steps" (Proverbs 16:9). God is a covenant-keeper; he keeps us as the pupil of his eye; he watches over us; he protects us as a mother bird hides her young under her wings, as stated in Psalm 17:8: "Keep me as the apple of your eye; hide me in the shadow of your wing." When I ponder these thoughts, an overwhelming gratitude to God swells from deep within, almost too much to contain.

The story continues. When Moses grew to manhood and saw his people suffering, he struck down the Egyptians, and Pharaoh sought him out to kill him, so he fled to the land of Midian. When

Moses saw that the shepherds were persecuting Zipporah for bringing water to the sheep, he helped his daughters bring water to the sheep.

Moses, as his name means, had a passion for rescuing those in need. He then married Zipporah, and they had two sons, and lived together in the wilderness of Midian for forty years. Therefore, he became the son-in-law of Zipporah's father, Reuel, and was given a podium and prepared to be the leader of Israel.

After the king of Egypt died, God called Moses from the flames of the bush at Mount Sinai and told him that he was sending him to lead his people, who were suffering at the hands of the Egyptians, to the land of Canaan, a land flowing with milk and honey.

Then Moses, knowing his weakness, said to God, "Who am I that I should go to Pharaoh and bring the children of Israel out of Egypt?" (Exodus 3:11). Moses may have answered God in a state of low self-esteem and not realizing the enormity of the God's power for a few seconds. At God's call, Moses hesitated because he knew he was weak.

I might speak God like this with boldness if I was Moses: "I lack strength and wisdom and feel uncertain about leading the Israelites. Yet, in God's might and as the King of kings, I am willing to try with your guidance."

What would you say to God? What is your answer?

So, let's move on to the story: God told Moses that he would need people like elders for the rescue of Israel, and God empowered Moses so that his staff would become a serpent, his hands would be healed of leprosy, and the Nile would become blood when it poured over the land. He told Moses to take the staff of power and use it to perform miracles of leprosy. And when Moses answered God, again he said that he couldn't do it because his mouth was stiff and dull, so he asked God to send someone else to do it. I can't begin to fathom how frustrated God must have been with Moses' ongoing reluctance.

Personal Exodus

God is so angry with Moses for pulling back and that he raises up Aaron, Moses' brother, who is well-spoken, to go help Moses in their deliverance:

> But Moses said, "Pardon your servant, Lord. Please send someone else." Then the Lord's anger burned against Moses, and he said, "What about your brother, Aaron the Levite? I know he can speak well. He is already on his way to meet you, and he will be glad to see you." (Exodus 4:13–14)

But most importantly, Moses faithfully carried out God's commands, listening carefully and unwaveringly to what God deemed most important. As a result he has been called the great man of God, considered the most important prophet in Christianity.

Moses and his first lieutenant, Aaron, return to Egypt and demand the freedom of the people from Pharaoh. Pharaoh, of course, refuses, and the Hebrew slaves suffer even more. The Hebrews become angry and resentful, mocking Moses and Aaron as their suffering intensifies. When Pharaoh's stubbornness shows no sign of abating, God sends the famous ten plagues. The first is described in Exodus 7:14, in which water, the source of life, is turned into blood, the symbol of death. The tenth, the death of the firstborn, is described in Exodus 12:29–31.

To further address the final plague, the annihilation of the firstborn, in order to protect the Hebrews' firstborn, God commanded Moses and Aaron to have the Hebrews paint lamb's blood on the doorposts of their homes. This was to ensure that the plagues of the night, which killed all the firstborn of the Egyptians, would pass right by the Hebrews' homes.

God also instructed the Hebrews to prepare unleavened bread as food, along with the meat of the animals they caught, in order to encourage them to leave Egypt in a hurry. This is the origin of the Jewish festival of Passover, or Pascha.

After the tenth plague killed his own son, Pharaoh gave up fighting against God and let all the Hebrews out of Egypt, allowing the Israelites to escape from Egypt. This is the plot of the Exodus, the partial story of how Moses led the Israelites out of Egypt.

Let's take a moment here to consider Pharaoh's stubbornness. An omnipotent God could have used his divine power to deliver the Israelites once and for all, in a different way, without using these ten plagues. He was patient with Pharaoh and even gave him a chance. But Pharaoh was too stubborn, too arrogant to change his mind, and the tenth plague brought him to his knees before God at the death of his own son.

Ten Commandments

At this time we will look deeper into the Ten Commandments, which are found in Exodus 20:3–17. Biblical scholars estimate that the Ten Commandments were given to the Israelites about five months after they left Egypt, based on Exodus 19:1: "In the third month that the children of Israel were in the land of Egypt, they came to the wilderness of Sinai."

In order to enter the Promised Land, a land flowing with milk and honey, Moses became the leader of the Israelites and wandered in the wilderness for forty years. The Ten Commandments were written by God on stone and given to Moses. They are as follows.

1. Do not serve any other gods besides God.
2. Do not make idols.
3. Do not take the name of God in vain.
4. Keep the Sabbath.
5. Honor your father and mother.
6. Do not murder.
7. Do not commit adultery.
8. Do not steal.
9. Do not bear false witness.
10. Do not covet what belongs to others.

Moses was given the law to stone people to death if they broke commandments 1–4, 6, or 7 above.

The most unusual of the Ten Commandments is the prohibition against idols. The Hebrews differed from other cultures in this regard. Most people's made statues or pictures of their gods, but the Hebrews believed that their god was an invisible spiritual being and could not be represented by man-made objects. Yet they broke this rule in their lives.

While Moses was receiving the Ten Commandments on the mountain, the Hebrews were making a golden calf and partying. Then Moses, coming down from the mountain, heard weird sounds from the camp down the hill. When Moses found out what people were doing in his absence, he got so angry at them (he might have said, "All of you inpatient and unfaithful people of Israel!!!") that he broke the tablets in half.

> 17 When Joshua heard the noise of the people shouting, he said to Moses, "There is the sound of war in the camp."
> 18 Moses replied:
> "It is not the sound of victory,
> > it is not the sound of defeat;
> > it is the sound of singing that I hear."
> 19 When Moses approached the camp and saw the calf and the dancing, his anger burned and he threw the tablets out of his hands, breaking them to pieces at the foot of the mountain. (Exodus 32:17–19)

Two Great Commandments

Now I would like to share with you the words of Jesus, who reinterprets the Ten Commandments in the New Testament. Jesus refocuses on the cross that Moses received and says to us, "For I did not come by law or by prophets to abolish it, but to fulfill it," as stated in Matthew 5:17–18: "Think not that I am come to destroy the law, or the prophets, or the kingdom of heaven: for I am not come to destroy, but to fulfill for verily I say unto you, Till heaven and earth pass away, one jot or one tittle shall not pass from the law, till all be fulfilled."

Jesus' interpretation of the Law's meaning from the basics to the details elevates the Law into a complete moral code.

First, Jesus' reinterpretation of the sixth commandment, "Thou shalt not commit adultery," and the seventh commandment, "Thou shalt not murder," appears in Matthew 5:21–48:

> Love thy neighbor and hate thine enemy. but I say unto you, love your enemies, and pray for them that persecute you. For if ye do these things, ye shall be the sons of your Father which is in heaven: for God maketh his sun to rise on the evil and on the good, and sends his rain on the just and on the unjust: and what reward hath any man, if ye love them that love you: neither doth the publican say, If ye do unto your brother, what shall ye do more than another: neither doth the Gentile. Be ye therefore perfect, even as your Father which is in heaven is perfect.

According to Jesus, not only do they apply behaviorally, but they also apply psychologically. For example, the commandment "Thou shalt not kill" includes anger, hatred, envy, and jealousy, all of which are the sources from which murder springs. As for adultery, Jesus explains that if people look at each other with lust, they have committed adultery in their hearts. This is a reinterpretation of the Law and the Ten Commandments.

Jesus spoke of the second commandment, "Love your neighbor as yourself." A rich young man came to Jesus and asked, "What shall I do to inherit eternal life? Jesus said, "If you want to enter into life, you must keep the commandments." The rich young man asked Jesus, "Which commandments?" Jesus only told him the fifth through tenth commandments. The rich young man said, "I have been keeping them since I was a child, so what do I lack?" Jesus said, "If you are so perfect, what do you lack?" (Matthew 19:16–22). If we interpret the words of Jesus from a different perspective, it might mean, "If you claim to be perfect, do you not realize your own shortcomings? What do you think is lacking in yourself?"

Then Jesus said, "If you are so perfect, go sell your possessions and give to the poor and follow me." This was Jesus' suggestion to the young man that he sell his possessions as proof that he truly loved his neighbor, but the young man hesitated and turned back. Here's a Bible passage that proves that Jesus thought he had kept the commandment to love your neighbor, but rich young man hadn't.

When Jesus was asked by a lawyer what was the greatest commandment in the Law, he condensed the Ten Commandments into two. The first commandment is to love the Lord your God with all your heart, and with all your soul, and with all your mind, and the second is to love your neighbor as yourself; and these two commandments are the whole law and the prophets, he declared.

God is the only good one in the world and, as we all know, we are all sinners, but by God's grace we are saved. Jesus paid our debt—our sins, my sins—on the cross and was laid in the tomb, and rose three days later. Therefore, God and us are a community, all connected and united. We are God's family, and all human beings are a precious expression of God's love.

Chapter 4

Commandments

Overlooked

WE WANT TO LOOK deeper into the Ten Commandments described in the previous chapter. These Commandments handed down to Moses on Mount Sinai are well known, but in contemporary times their significance is often overlooked, and not appreciated. In the Gospel of Mark Jesus says,

> "The most important one," answered Jesus, "is this: 'Hear, O Israel: The Lord our God, the Lord is one. Love the Lord your God with all your heart and with all your soul and with all your mind and with all your strength.' The second is this: 'Love your neighbor as yourself.' There is no commandment greater than these." (Mark 12:29–31)

Jesus condensed the Ten Commandments into two great commandments: to love God with all your heart and with all your strength and to love your neighbor as yourself.

God gave us these commandments as a rule of love. There exist ten divine commandments, yet when examining their biblical interconnections, they ultimately converge into one central theme: love. It's all about love. Therefore, rather than simply reading all the

Commandments, infuse love at the beginning of each one to enhance understanding. May God's guidance inspire and strengthen everyone to faithfully adhere to these commandments, bringing hope and purpose to our lives.

#1. God is greater than anything else and He is the only one who is all-powerful. God, the greatest in the world and the universe, stands unmatched in His power and majesty. His sovereignty knows no equal, and His teachings emphasize His singular supremacy. In His wisdom, He reveals the truth: there are no other gods beside Him. He alone reigns as the one true God, deserving of all reverence and worship.

If riches, greed, self, power, honor, pleasure, people, or any other things are more important to you than God, then you have other gods:

> No one can serve two masters. Either you will hate the one and love the other, or you will be devoted to the one and despise the other. You cannot serve both God and money. (Matthew 6:24)
>
> ... for they loved human praise more than praise from God. (John 12:43)
>
> Put to death, therefore, whatever belongs to your earthly nature: sexual immorality, impurity, lust, evil desires and greed, which is idolatry. (Colossians 3:5)
>
> Without love, unforgiving, slanderous, without self-control, brutal, not lovers of the good, treacherous, rash, conceited, lovers of pleasure rather than lovers of God. (2 Timothy 3:3–4)

—*If you love God, do not serve any other gods beside God.*

#2. In Exodus 32, the Israelites at the foot of the mountain were impatient while Moses spent forty days fasting, being with God, and receiving the Ten Commandments. Then, perhaps out of anxiety, they cried out to Aaron to make a god of their own because Moses hadn't come down from the mountain and they didn't know what was going on.

Aaron, Moses' right-hand man, was weak in faith and in the idea of completing the task as second leader. The brother of Moses and a Levite, one of the groups of priests, he gave in to the people's demands and made a new god, a golden calf, out of all the gold and silver they had brought with them, and he called out to the people to build an altar and worship it.

The Bible doesn't indicate it, but had Aaron, the priest, forgotten the power of God's ten plagues on Pharaoh in Egypt? Had he lost his mind completely? Perhaps he hadn't forgotten, but rather sought to exploit Moses' absence to assume leadership?

In our world, even in our churches, when confronted with adversity, we instinctively seek solace through various means. Individuals often indulge in immediate comforts, fostering a fleeting sense of solace. Is it a new car that lifts your spirits? Perhaps the embrace of favorite garments or a sip of alcohol? What are the ephemeral sources of solace you turn to? Can we inadvertently elevate anything in this world to the status of an idol?

We must wait for Moses, however long it takes. We must wait with patience in prayer to God. Wait for our eternal comfort. God says in Exodus 34:14, "Do not worship any other god, for the Lord, whose name is Jealous, is a jealous God." God wants His people who belong to Him to not fall under someone else's spell. As our Creator and Father, God knows what is best for us, loves us, guides us, and protects us. He longs for us to be safe in His arms. That is the jealousy God speaks of.

—If you love the God's sacred image, you shall not make yourself an idol.

 # 3. Today's some Christian care more for their own religious traditions than the commands of God. This same problem is plaguing the church today. Many have taken His name but have no interest in learning and for The Bible warns against hypocrisy in Matthew 7:21, emphasizing that merely attending church and professing Christianity with words will not secure entry into the kingdom of heaven.

True acceptance depends on conformity to the will of the heavenly Father. Hypocrites, in this context, are those who lack a wholehearted love for God, neglect to live by His Word, and avoid walking in His ways. Instead, they attend church as a mere formality and follow their own ideas.

In today's world, Even call itself Christian not going to churches, numerous people don't honor the God, lack knowledge of God, and fail to live by His teachings. All while identifying themselves as Christians. Their focus is often on religious traditions rather than on obeying God's commands. This challenge persists in today's churches, where many bear His name but show little interest in understanding and following His way.

> Not everyone who says to me, 'Lord, Lord,' will not enter the kingdom of heaven, but only the one who does the will of my Father who is in heaven. (Matthew 7:21)

—If you love God's name, you shall not misuse the name of the LORD your God.

#4. Keeping the Sabbath holy means doing our best to remember Him throughout the day. It is the story of the life we live, day by day, in what we do and how we live it. And Sunday, or the Sabbath day, is a day to prepare for. If you take the day off from Friday to go to a rave party or watch TV all night and make your body too busy and tired, how can you keep Sunday holy?

Observing holiness involves our constant effort to remember Him in our daily lives. It unfolds in the narrative of our existence, reflected in our actions and the manner in which we lead our lives each day. Sunday, or the Sabbath day, holds a special significance that requires preparation. We can all go to church, worship God, and learn how to be better people and Christians.

—If you love the seventh day, remember the Sabbath by keeping it holy.

#5. In the intricate era of life, our parents emerge as an unwavering guiding light of unconditional love after God. Recognizing and honoring someone naturally evokes a sense of humility, and for me, expressing love and respect for my parents involves more than just words. It's a conscious act of humility—bowing my head in gratitude for the profound gift of life they bestowed upon me.

Displaying respect for our parents takes on diverse forms, as each relationship is unique. It could involve actively listening to their stories, sharing quality time, or providing assistance when needed. Beyond the daily gestures, it's essential to acknowledge the sacrifices they made and the challenges they navigated to nurture and raise us. Their sleepless nights when we were just a baby and as we matured, the merest hint of discomfort would soften their hearts, mirroring our own agony. They'd trudge to their jobs, thinking about their children's happy faces, toiling relentlessly until their very bones bowed and contorted. Despite their hunger, witnessing their children eat brought them a feast of joy, filling their own bellies with contentment.

Our parents' love and care serve as the foundation upon which we build our lives. Therefore, reciprocating that love involves a continuous effort to understand their perspectives, support their endeavors, and be a source of comfort when they need it. In essence, demonstrating respect becomes an ongoing commitment to fostering a bond that goes beyond familial ties to a relationship built on mutual understanding, appreciation, and enduring love. Therefore, we can understand that the love and care shown by our parents are reflections of God's love, encouraging us to care for those who have cared for us first.

—*If you love your parents, honor your father and your mother.*

#6. As I begin this, I want to unfold the story using life as an example. Beyond humans, this world is teeming with entities that possess plant and animal life. Just imagine that at one time, during our stroll, we came across a nameless wildflower lying on the road. If that small, grass-like flower seemed lovely and beautiful, would you feel the urge to end its life? Similarly, if an unnamed insect appeared too cute, cuddly, and adorable, would you consider taking away its life? Absolutely not. Especially considering that humanity, the lord of all things, would have such inclinations if possessed by a loving heart?

—*If you love life, you shall not murder.*

#7. As we all know, an adulterer is an individual who voluntarily engages in a sexual relationship with a person outside the sacred bounds of marriage who is not his or her spouse. It is an act of betrayal between a married person and that breaks a promise to a spouse and inflicts deep wounds on him or her. And that breaks a person's trust, pride, and basic human principles and causes mental anguish that leads to great sorrow.

Furthermore, betrayal between friends, parents, siblings, and relationships, even if it is not between a couple, produces a mental pain that lingers for a long time, possibility staying with a person for the rest of his or her lifetime. Synonyms for "faithfulness" are fidelity, loyalty, constancy, devotion, trueness, true-heartedness, dedication, commitment, allegiance, adherence, dependability. It serves as a poignant of the values essential for the harmony of human connections.

The connection between "full of faith" and "faithful" is related to the idea of being steadfast and loyal in one's beliefs or commitments. In essence, faithfulness boils down to trust, reliance, and a commitment equal fundamental to love.

—*If you love faithfulness, you shall not commit adultery.*

#8. Stealing something from another person is an invasion of that person's personal privacy, a lack of respect for the person who stole it, and a crime. When an unauthorized person takes something that belongs to the owner without permission, it is also a violation of the rights of others to gain an advantage. It is also interpreted to mean to deceive. Exodus 22:1–5, 14–15 states,

> Whoever steals an ox or a sheep and slaughters it or sells it must pay back five head of cattle for the ox and four sheep for the sheep. If a thief is caught breaking in at night and is struck by a fatal blow, the defender is not guilty of bloodshed; but if it happens after sunrise, the defender is guilty of bloodshed.
>
> Anyone who steals must certainly take restitution, but if they have nothing, they must be sold to pay for their theft. If the stolen animal is found alive in their possession—whether ox or donkey or sheep—they must pay back double. If anyone grazes their livestock in a field or vineyard and lets them stray and they graze in someone else's field, the offender must make restitution from the best of their own field or vineyard . . .
>
> If anyone borrows an animal from their neighbor and it is injured or dies while the owner is not present, they must make restitution. But if the owner is with the animal, the borrower will not have to pay. If the animal was hired, the money paid for the hire covers the loss.

The word "steal"/"theft" refer to the act of carrying off by stealth that which is not one's own to sweep away, to take secretly, to deceive. Stealing can be both physical and mental. Stealing is the act of an unauthorized person taking something that belongs to a neighbor without the owner's permission.

In this context, "neighbor's possessions" relate to property: money, male and female servants, clothing, livestock, grain, and spoils. Taking someone else's money and not paying it back is also stealing. Secretly defrauding others is also stealing.

Even if it's not money, it's also stealing to take advantage of others by tricking them into a trap with secret thoughts and devious plans. What others have, what they have earned, should be celebrated together by recognizing their passion, time, and energy they put into it.

Even beyond mere currency, exploiting others through cunning schemes and covert intentions is akin to theft, as stated in Genesis 31:7: "yet your father has cheated me by changing my wages ten times. However, God has not allowed him to harm me."

Genuine appreciation for what others possesses, acknowledging the dedication, time, and effort they have invested, is the true celebration of their achievements.

—*If you love the possessions of others, you shall not steal.*

#9. What is a lie? A lie, according to the Merriam-Webster dictionary, is an assertion knowingly or believed by the speaker to be untrue, with the intent to deceive. Lies are inherently valueless, being untrue statements and a form of deception tantamount to fraud. Motivations for lying vary, such as serving one's self-interest or inflicting harm on others, often stemming from low self-esteem to evade uncomfortable situations. In Matthew 15:17–20 Jesus states,

> Don't you see that whatever enters the mouth goes into the stomach and then out of the body? But the things that come out of a person's mouth come from the heart, and these defile them. For out of the heart come evil thoughts—murder, adultery, sexual immorality, theft, false testimony, slander. These are what defile a person; but eating with unwashed hands does not defile them.

Jesus emphasizes that the impurity comes not from what enters the mouth but from what emerges, highlighting the importance of controlling the tongue and mouth by mastering the heart.

Therefore, lying is designated as a prohibited behavior because it brings remorse to the conscience of the person telling the lie, and the lie causes harm, causing both parties to suffer. So why do people lie? Most of the time, people who lie have low self-esteem and want to look good to others, so in order to satisfy the other person, they say what they think they want to hear.

—If you love truth, you shall not give false testimony against your neighbor.

#10. Coveting entails feeling intense jealousy or envy for something someone else possesses, desperately. This destructive emotion not only leads to personal misery but also hinders placing God at the forefront of one's priorities. This commandment serves as a safeguard, preventing individuals from succumbing to the pitfalls of this detrimental habit.

When I feel jealous of something, there's room for it to be positive because I can work toward it, I can aim for it, and I can become better at it. But because the focus of envy is on someone else, it's seen as something I can't control, so it tends to boil down to putting others down or getting frustrated with yourself if you are jealous of someone else's accomplishments.

—If you love contentment, you shall not covet.

In conclusion, at the beginning of this chapter, Jesus' condensed the Ten Commandments into two: love God and love your neighbor as yourself. It is my conviction that when we read the above commandments with the word "love" in front of them, it enhances their clarity and makes them easier to keep. These commandments are presented as laws, but they can be seen as simple behaviors rooted in love that are accessible to all of us.

We can all act based on love, as stated in 1 Corinthians 13:4–7: "Love is patient and kind; love does not envy or boast; it is not arrogant or rude. It does not insist on its own way; it is not irritable or resentful. It does not rejoice at wrongdoing but rejoices with the truth. Love bears all things, believes all things, hopes all things, endures all things." Therefore, under the gentle guidance of the Holy Spirit, we wholeheartedly immerse ourselves in the sacred teachings of God, delving into the depths of His unyielding love and boundless grace. It is through this profound understanding that we nurture the hope of one day standing as radiant witnesses, shining forth the brilliance of God's infinite love to the world, as stated in Acts 1:8: "but you will receive power when the Holy Spirit comes on you; and you will be my witnesses in Jerusalem, and in all Judea and Samaria, and to the ends of the earth."

Chapter 5

United

Fun in Marriage

IN THE PAST, AN unexpected conversation unfolded with a colleague at work. She excitedly mentioned organizing a highly intriguing Friday party with five or six couples attending. The pure joy radiating from her face as she spoke piqued my curiosity. I was captivated by the story and prompted her to continue.

    And she continued to speak with an enthusiastic smile on her face, "Can you guess what kind of party it is?" I replied with deep intrigue, "With that radiant, joyful smile, it sounds like something quite remarkable!" Her enthusiasm became more evident as she continued talking. "Well, we call it 'couple dancing.' Essentially, we exchange partners and spend the night with a different couple each week."

    After hearing about the party, I was so shocked I almost fell backwards from the unexpected disclosure. It made me wonder if I was living in a modern-day Sodom and Gomorrah. With a displeased expression, I addressed my colleague, "Wouldn't that be inappropriate, potentially causing infidelity and jealousy?" But with a sense of misunderstanding written all over her face, she said, "No, it's to prevent infidelity and potential divorces. You don't need to worry about jealousy due to our long-standing friendships. It's just a safe and enjoyable game." In this way she expressed disagreement with my comment.

Where did her decision that it's just a safe and enjoyable game come from? I wondered if there was a sudden realization. I speculated about who might have initially recommended such a game to play and how that person might have also found it wrong and awkward at first.

Habits have either immediate or latent rewards. Those with immediate rewards are easier to acquire, while those with delayed rewards are harder to maintain. Consequently, engaging in an immediate reward, like checking messages on the phone, is easier than working out.

In my opinion, the Friday party of my colleague seems to have formed a legitimacy in their brain as a habit that easily provides immediate rewards. I cannot find any evidence supporting the legitimacy of their Friday "couple dance." However, evidence against it can be found in the Bible. The party of the colleague involves humans mutually engaging in immorality. In other words, it's collective immorality. Wouldn't it feel filthy and leave a foul taste in your mouth?

We all can see if we look at the Bible, as stated in 1 Corinthians 7:3–5, that husbands are to fulfill their obligations to their wives, and wives are to do the same to their husbands:

> Husbands should fulfill their marital duty to their wives, and wives should also do the same for their husbands. The wife does not have authority over her own body but yields it to her husband. In the same way, the husband does not have authority over his own body but yields it to his wife. Do not deprive each other except perhaps by mutual consent and for a time, so that you may devote yourselves to prayer. Then come together again so that Satan will not tempt you because of your lack of self-control.

Culture in Society

Before diving into the biblical verses about Sodom and Gomorrah in Genesis 19, let's briefly summarize Genesis 18. Abraham, sitting at the entrance of his tent under the shade of the trees of Mamre, lifted his eyes and saw three men standing nearby, disguised as travelers, two angels and God in human form, putting Himself lower as a humble human. Hastening toward them, Abraham bowed down to the ground and offered hospitality, pleading to them not to pass by but to receive his kindness. He asked them to rest and wash their feet while he fetched water. Then he invited them to eat and rest under the tree. Curious about their visit, Abraham eagerly requested them to stay.

Hurrying into the tent, Abraham instructed his wife Sarah to prepare bread. He selected a fine calf and instructed the servants to quickly prepare a meal. He then served curds and milk to the three visitors and watched as they ate.

God asked, "Where is your wife, Sarah?" Abraham replied, "She is inside the tent." Then God said to Abraham, "I will surely return to you about this time next year, and Sarah, your wife, will have a son." Sarah was eavesdropping on the entrance to the tent. Abraham and Sarah were very old, and Sarah was well past the age of childbearing.

Upon hearing this, Sarah couldn't help but laugh to herself, thinking, "After I am worn out and my lord is old, will I now have this pleasure?" God said to Abraham, "Why did Sarah laugh and say, 'Will I really have a child, now that I am old?' Is anything too hard for the Lord? I will return it to you at the appointed time next year, and Sarah will have a son." Sarah denied laughing, saying, "I did not laugh." God replied, "Yes, you did laugh" (Genesis 18:9–10).

In this account, there might have been a moment of doubt mixed with joy in Sarah's elderly self, wondering if she could bear a child. When Sarah denied laughing, God wasn't angry with Sarah, but he simply responded, "Yes, you did laugh." From a personal perspective, this statement might have been delivered with a humorous smile.

After receiving hospitality from Abraham, they gazed toward Sodom, and God said, "Shall I hide from Abraham what I am about to do? Abraham will surely become a great and powerful nation, and all nations on earth will be blessed through him."

God continued, "The outcry against Sodom and Gomorrah is so great and their sin so grievous that I will go down and see what's going on in those cities, if what they have done is as bad as the outcry that has reached me." Abraham approached God and asked, "Will you sweep away the righteous with the wicked? What if there are fifty righteous people in the city? Will you really sweep it away?" God said, "If I find fifty righteous people in the city, I will spare the whole place for their sake."

Abraham pleaded again, "Now that I have been so bold as to speak to the Lord, what if only forty are found there or thirty, twenty, ten?" God replied, "For the sake of forty or less to ten righteous people, I will not do it."

This dialogue between God and Abraham reveals Abraham's compassionate nature toward the lives in Sodom and Gomorrah. His fervent plea to spare the cities incase if a small number of righteous individuals existed is evident in their conversation.

Shameful Lusts

Why did Sodom and Gomorrah face such a devastating judgment? What sin led to their destruction? Commonly, people attribute the sin of Sodom and Gomorrah to sexual depravity. The term "sodomy" is derived from Sodom, depicting sexually corrupted practices, including abnormal sexual acts such as homosexual behavior, as stated in Genesis 19:4-5: "Before they had gone to bed, all the men from every part of the city of Sodom—both young and old—surrounded the house. They called to Lot, 'Where are the men who came to you tonight? Bring them out to us so that we can have sex with them.'"

From the above biblical passage, when the two angels entered Lot's house, the residents of Sodom gathered that night, regardless of age, demanding to have relations with the guests. Even after Lot offered his two daughters instead of the guests, they refused. They violently tried to break down the door and forcefully bring out the angels.

The following Bible verses explain shameful acts of unnatural relations

> Because of this, God gave them over to shameful lusts. Even their women exchanged natural sexual relations for unnatural ones. In the same way the men also abandoned natural relations with women and were inflamed with lust for one another. Men committed shameful acts with other men and received in themselves the due penalty for their error. (Romans 1:26–27)

Their actions depicted a rejection of the natural order established by God between men and women, seeking pleasure in aberrant sexual desires. The sexual depravity of Sodom not only violated the principle of offering absolute protection to guests but also manifested societal corruption by openly engaging in collective wickedness.

Sodom and Gomorrah faced judgment due to sexual depravity. So, what is the current state of sexual ethics in our country? In TV dramas, infidelity often seems more enticing than normal love stories. Even the sexual misconduct of influential figures is sometimes reported in the media. The prevalent immoral sexual culture in society remains a concern. Although it's decreased significantly, issues like sexual harassment and violence persist within workplaces.

Sexuality is a gift from God and beautiful, but it requires restraint and boundaries in all aspects. Unrestrained sexuality can be perilous. However, confining the severity of sexual issues merely to Sodom and Gomorrah's judgment diminishes the gravity of the problem. Sexual depravity is a visible manifestation, but the more fundamental issue lies in the widespread injustice and lawlessness in society.

In Genesis 19:13, the two angels explicitly state, "The outcry against them is so great before the Lord that he has sent us to destroy it." In 18:20, God had already said to Abraham, "The outcry against Sodom and Gomorrah is so great and their sin so grievous."

The term "outcry" denotes a cry to God's court by those who have suffered unjustly or are vulnerable due to unlawful acts that God surely answers. Another Bible verses depicts Abel, killed by Cain, crying out to God: "The Lord said, 'What have you done? Listen! Your brother's blood cries out to me from the ground'" (Genesis 4:10). And Exodus 2:23–24 describes something similar: "The Israelites groaned in their slavery and cried out, and their cry for help because of their slavery went up to God."

Grant Me Justice

In the Gospel of Luke, a parable describes a widow who, every day, cries out to an unjust judge and says, "'Grant me justice against my adversary'" (18:3). Jesus shared this parable and asked, "Will not God grant justice to his chosen ones who cry to him day and night?" (18:7).

One must not treat others unjustly, for if someone is wronged, they will appeal directly to God. When a society wrongs people, that cry reaches the gates of heaven. We know that God listens keenly to the sighs of the weak.

The fact that Sodom and Gomorrah became societies devoid of compassion for the weak might have echoed louder in God's ears than their sexual depravity. In consequence, they might have steered toward destruction by sulfur. When the angels, as strangers, came, they didn't show consideration but instead tried to violently break into Lot's house and demanded the strangers be brought out.

> They called to Lot, "Where are the men who came to you tonight? Bring them out to us so that we can have sex with them." Lot went outside to meet them and shut the door behind him and said, "No, my friends. Don't

do this wicked thing. Look, I have two daughters who have never slept with a man. Let me bring them out to you, and you can do what you like with them. But don't do anything to these men, for they have come under the protection of my roof." (Genesis 19:5–8)

In the above Bible verses, the manifestation of sexual depravity is seen as a result of a society losing its traditions and regulations, spiraling into madness. It signifies the absence of values and traditions that hold such a society together. Society has become materially affluent, yet it has destroyed all its spiritual foundations.

We've become a society that emphasizes material power over notions of respect, reverence, morality, order, and justice. It's as if we've become physically obese but mentally immature and lacking in self-control, suffering from a form of mental obesity where lack of mental control leads to the inability to restrain sexual debauchery.

The sexual depravity of Sodom and Gomorrah, from another perspective, demonstrates a lack of respect for individual dignity and life, transforming into a society driven by selfish desires even at the expense of resorting to violence. If they attempted such actions against angels, how rampant might have been unjust deaths or assaults in those cities?

Living in an unjust world like Sodom and Gomorrah, Lot might have constantly faced conflicts due to his different perspective and upright stance. He opposed their wicked actions of intending harm to the guests and was met with resistance, as stated in Genesis 19:9: "'Get out of our way,' they replied. 'This fellow came here as a foreigner, and now he wants to play the judge! We'll treat you worse than them.' They kept bringing pressure on Lot and moved forward to break down the do."

It is impressive to see the wicked words of the people of those cities. Listen to the evil talk in these verses. Lot, though living as a foreigner among them, was distinct from the people there. He knew God and His laws. Consequently, he didn't conform to the lifestyle of Sodom and Gomorrah, living righteously amidst their displeasure.

Had Lot compromised with their way of life, they might not have treated him in such a manner. Even when families from the same lineage meet, believers and non-believers have different values and standards. The world values boasting about house sizes, children, material possessions, and status. However, for believers, pride lies in the cross and the Word of God.

If you truly believe in Jesus, occasionally you might hear phrases like, "He has come to be our judge." Being among the righteous makes it easier to act righteously, while being among the wicked might incline one toward evil. Whom I befriend influences who I become. Associating with faithful believers leads to growing in faith, while befriending those indulging in vices leads to similar behavior. When your friends are all drunk, guess what? You're likely drunk too. Surround yourself with gamblers? You'll find yourself gambling. You often become a reflection of those you spend time with.

If one of my colleagues mistakes a party full of sin for a delightful, joyous occasion, they're no different from the people of Sodom and Gomorrah. Consequently, they might fail to recognize the good conscience God has instilled within them. When guilt seeps in, seek the help of the Holy Spirit and choose to cease those actions, opting to step away from such situations.

> Be alert and of sober mind. Your enemy the devil prowls around like a roaring lion looking for someone to devour. Resist him, standing firm in the faith, because you know that the family of believers throughout the world is undergoing the same kind of sufferings. (1 Peter 5:8–9)

In the above verse, the apostle Peter is so right about believers' sufferings, which continue from thousands of years ago to now. God instructs on how to resist the devil: "Blessed is the one who does not walk in step with the wicked or stand in the way that sinners take or sit in the company of mockers" (Psalm 1:1). Even while living in this world, we should always be with the righteous community of Jesus. The church is that community where we find comfort, are challenged, and gain new strength to live a blessed and righteous life in the world. Are you currently in God's grace, experiencing spiritual blessings in Christ?

Therefore, in this world, at the place where the narrow gate and the wide intersect, some people choose the wide gate and enter through it, walking along the wide path to destruction. And yet, some people choose the narrow gate and walk along the narrow path. Truly, God will always guide us when we seek His help through prayer. Throughout our lives, we often face a multitude of decisions, each presenting us with the choice between the wide path and the narrow path.

What is the wide path?

The wide path represents the entry point for those who reject the acknowledgment of Jesus as the Son of God and have a lack belief in Him. It serves as the entrance to a path that unfolds into a vast, comfortable route, luring many with its sense of ease. This expansive pathway is adorned with numerous delights, making it an enjoyable stroll where one can revel in amusement. It's often favored by many for its seemingly care-free and limited to only pleasurable journey. Jesus says in Matthew 7:13-14, "Enter through the narrow gate. For wide is the gate and broad is the road that leads to destruction, and many enter through it. But small is the gate and narrow the road that leads to life, and only a few find it."

If you continue reading Bible verses reads you may encounter people traveling through the wide gate, such as false prophets and wolves in sheep's clothing. Jesus explains that their actions result in their fruit:

> Watch out for false prophets. They come to you in sheep's clothing, but inwardly they are ferocious wolves. By their fruit you will recognize them. Do people pick grapes from thornbushes, or figs from thistles? Likewise, every good tree bears good fruit, but a bad tree bears bad fruit. A good tree cannot bear bad fruit, and a bad tree cannot bear good fruit. Every tree that does not bear good fruit is cut down and thrown into the fire. Thus, by their fruit you will recognize them. (Matthew 7:15-20)

United

It's important for each of us to reflect on our relationship and ascertain our identities as who we are in Jesus Christ, striving to be more like Him as we journey through our path, and continuously asking the Holy Spirit to guide us.

Chapter 6

The Veil of Soul

Eunuchs

I'VE MET TWO SINGLE individuals in the past. One was a woman my age and from the same area I lived, whom I met through the local church's district services. The other was much older than I and worked at the same workplace. Over time, we built a friendship and got to know each other gradually. As we grew closer and our friendship deepened, personal questions naturally came up.

The woman my age moved from Canada and was a sharp-minded woman acknowledged enough at her job for the company to sponsor her American citizenship application. She had an average build and appearance, but she had a clean mind akin to that of a child.

I have been married previously, and she believed I had somewhat expert experience in matters of dating. One day, based on this assumption, she posed a question to me with hopeful expression: "How can I meet a decent guy?" I'm not an expert counselor, but I replied, "Well, meeting someone destined by God, where and how it happens, that's something I can't definitively say."

She grew serious, confiding, "Honestly, there's a guy at work I like, but it seems he doesn't see me as a romantic prospect." Sensing her uncertainty, I offered some advice: "Perhaps it's time to refine your approach. Try enhancing your appearance with makeup and stylish attire. See how he reacts." Her response caught me off guard, revealing her innocence in matters of the heart. "No, I'll start wearing makeup when I find the right man to marry."

Determined to broaden her perspective, I gently nudged her toward a more open-minded outlook. "You're approaching this from the wrong angle. Begin by presenting yourself well and meeting new people. As you grow closer, the little details won't matter as much."

It appeared that she struggled to grasp my point. Typically, men tend to focus outwardly, especially on appearance when meeting women. Creating an initial spark of interest in that direction is crucial to capturing their attention. Just like a beautifully adorned outside-of-the-box item signals customers to make a purchase, "liking" signifies positive feelings or interest between individuals.

Married or Not

When a man starts to like a woman, these feelings manifest in various ways, often conveyed through subtle signals we might not consciously perceive. Both women were well into their adulthood, considering marriage and developing an interest, but they had never really had a formal date with a proper man before, nor had they ever held hands. Let's look at a Bible passage regarding the matter of marriage.

> The Pharisees came to Jesus, testing him and asking, "Is it lawful for a man to divorce his wife for any and every reason?" Jesus replied, "Haven't you read that at the beginning, the Creator made them male and female, and said, 'For this reason, a man will leave his father and mother and be united to his wife, and the two will become one flesh'? So, they are no longer two, but one flesh. Therefore, what God has joined together, let no one separate." "Why then," they asked, "did Moses command that a man give his wife a certificate of divorce and send her

> away?" Jesus replied, "Moses permitted you to divorce your wives because your hearts were hard. But it was not this way from the beginning. I tell you that anyone who divorces his wife, except for sexual immorality, and marries another woman commits adultery." The disciples said to him, "If this is the situation between a husband and wife, it is better not to marry." Jesus replied, "Not everyone can accept this word, but only those to whom it has been given. For there are eunuchs who were born that way, and there are eunuchs who have been made eunuchs by others—and there are those who choose to live like eunuchs for the sake of the kingdom of heaven. The one who can accept this should accept it."

In this passage above, which has three categories of eunuchs described by Jesus, the phrase "It is better not to marry" could be construed as "It is better for us not to marry, whether man or woman." My definition of of this type of eunuch is individuals, both men and women, who choose not to be fruitful and multiply or opt not to follow the divine command of Genesis 1:28, where God commands, "Be fruitful and increase in number; fill the earth and subdue it."

Which of these three eunuchs do my friends think they belong to? They have certainly surpassed the typical marriageable age, have the desire to marry, yet have never met a man in their lives. One of my friends, who was of my age, I couldn't see each other due to my relocation, and the older one fought colon cancer for about five years before passing away at the age of sixty-five. Given these examples, particularly with the older colleague, I speculate she might belong to those "born that way," eunuchs from birth.

History of Castrato

The Bible contains verses about various eunuchs. In Daniel 1:3 there is the eunuch Ashpenaz of the Babylonian kingdom. Ester mentions, "When Esther's female attendants and eunuchs came and told her about Mordecai, she was in great distress. She sent clothes

The Veil of Soul

for him to put on instead of his sackcloth, but he would not accept them" (Esther 4:4). Then there is the eunuch from Ethiopia in Acts 8:27: "So he started out, and on his way, he met an Ethiopian eunuch, an important official in charge of all the treasury of the Kandake (which means 'queen of the Ethiopians'). This man had gone to Jerusalem to worship." Through these verses, it's evident that eunuchs have existed since ancient times.

In the musical realm of Italy, there was a practice of castrating young boys before they reached puberty to create male singers called "castrati." This was a product of an era when women were prohibited from singing in churches, and later these individuals performed in operas as well.

A castrati had a very high voice, the effect that was produced either through castration or because of some hormonal problem. As a male opera singer, he sang as a soprano. In sixteenth-to-eigtheenth-century Italy, it was quite common to castrate boys who had exceptional singing abilities. If castration occurred before puberty, the usual effects of puberty wouldn't occur.

That includes the vocal cords enlarging and the voice getting deeper consequently. Castration before or during puberty prevents the voice from undergoing the typical physiological changes of maturation. As a result, they retain prepubescent vocal qualities and grow into adulthood in a unique way.

Although castration was illegal in many parts of Italy, it was often performed. Many poor families castrated their children because they believed it might provide better opportunities in the future. However, only a chosen few succeeded in attaining both wealth and fame for themselves, but the remainder did not achieve their ambitions. Over one hundred thousand boys underwent unthinkable actions against nature through castration, and the castrati were hired by churches to sing Gospels.

Then are these adults physically mature but with voices like children? Have you heard their singing?

Following castration, boys' bodies were tall, undergoing lengthening of their arms and legs due to the stop in the production of the male hormone testosterone, leading to a deficiency in masculine musculature. Understanding the history of castrati, some of people may express that their singing is beautiful, but when I listened to their singing, their voices sounded hauntingly sad, heart-breaking, as if hollowed from within and delivered with a trembling voice. These deeply sorrowful singers were born from an incredibly sad story of an insatiable chase after human desires, as these individuals were forcibly castrated to serve as opera singers and support their families.

Returning to the Bible, let's examine a verse fron the apostle Pau: "I say to the unmarried and to widows: It is good for them if they remain even as I am" (1 Corinthians 7:8). Paul lived alone for the sake of Jesus. He's the example of a eunuch for the sake of the kingdom of heaven. Therefore, the phrase "for the sake of the kingdom of heaven" likely refers not to the physical removal of reproductive organs but to those who, like the apostle Paul, dedicate their lives solely to Jesus, without seeking offspring, avoiding marriage and serving only Jesus.

The apostle Paul suggested it's better not to marry to avoid entanglements. He wasn't directly addressing the issue of marriage but rather the entanglement that diverts one's heart from God. Our hearts should belong to God alone. If married, it's easy for the heart to become entangled with the spouse since couples are always together, sharing life's moments.

During this, the heart may get entangled with the spouse, causing issues in departing from worldly matters toward God. The apostle Paul indicated that not being entangled through marriage leads to a life more aligned with the God's will on earth. He suggested it's better not to marry to avoid entanglements.

God's Command

Marriage is a divine mandate according to numerous Bible verses, a few of which are listed below.

> Therefore a man shall leave his father and mother and be joined to his wife, and they shall become one flesh. (Genesis 2:24)

> Likewise, husbands, live with your wives in an understanding way, showing honor to the woman as the weaker vessel, since they are heirs with you of the grace of life, so that your prayers may not be hindered. (1 Peter 3:7)
>
> But because of the temptation to sexual immorality, each man should have his own wife and each woman her own husband. (1 Corinthians 7:2)

The apostle Paul emphasizes the necessity to divert one's heart from the world toward God. This attitude suggests that not being entangled through marriage is preferable, as it avoids entanglement of the heart. If the heart becomes entangled with the world, one cannot follow Jesus toward the kingdom of heaven. Whether married or unmarried, the entanglement of the heart remains a problem. First Corinthians 7:26–38 states:

> I think that in view of the present distress it is good for a person to remain as he is. Are you bound to a wife? Do not seek to be free. Are you free from a wife? Do not seek a wife. But if you do marry, you have not sinned, and if a betrothed woman marries, she has not sinned. Yet those who marry will have worldly troubles, and I would spare you that. This is what I mean, brothers: the appointed time has grown very short. From now on, let those who have wives live as though they had none, and those who mourn as though they were not mourning, and those who rejoice as though they were not rejoicing, and those who buy as though they had no goods, and those who deal with the world as though they had no dealings with it.
>
> For the present form of this world is passing away. I want you to be free from anxieties. The unmarried man is anxious about the things of the Lord, how to please the Lord. But the married man is anxious about worldly things, how to please his wife, and his interests are divided. And the unmarried or betrothed woman is anxious about the things of the Lord, how to be holy in body and spirit. But the married woman is anxious about worldly things, how to please her husband.

> I say this for your own benefit, not to lay any restraint upon you, but to promote good order and to secure your undivided devotion to the Lord. If anyone thinks that he is not behaving properly toward his betrothed, if his passions are strong, and it has to be, let him do as he wishes would let them marry—it is no sin. But whoever is firmly established in his heart, being under no necessity but having his desire under control, and has determined this in his heart, to keep her as his betrothed, he will do well. So, then he who marries his betrothed does well, and he who refrains from marriage will do even better.

Summarizing these points, the apostle Paul's sole concern was the love of God. The way to love God was by diverting the heart toward Jesus and the path to heaven. If a spouse hinders this, not marrying is better. Conversely, if the lack of a spouse leads to entanglement through desires, then marrying is better.

Comparing entanglement through burning desires without marriage and entanglement with a spouse, there's a difference in the degree of entanglement. Being entangled with a spouse is better than being ensnared by desires. However, both entanglements hinder the heart's journey toward God. It's important to note that the Scriptures offer guidance rather than imposing restrictions.

Burning Desire

More specifically, it's about being tied to burning desires, being mentally anchored to earthly concerns, and teetering on the brink of immorality. Instead, it suggests that if lust becomes a significant hindrance to the journey toward God, then marriage, as a lesser entanglement, might be considered per the Bible.

As time passed, thoughts about the two women I had met previously crossed my mind. Though their thoughts were their own. There were moments where I felt a certain purity, freed from sins, emanating from their characters because they did not have marriage.

Furthermore, on my wedding day, I experienced something amazing that I want to share. For me, it may be a bit four-dimensional.

It was the moment when we stood before the officiant, Bible in hand, exchanged vows, made promises, and made our marriage official. As the invisible veil that had separated my husband and I, a beautiful ethereal curtain that allowed light to pass through, descended from heaven, I felt as if a white veil had been lifted from our souls.

There were people who solemnly stood as witnesses to our union on that unforgettable day, amidst a picturesque setting adorned with delicate white lace draping from rustic wooden beams, and fragrant blooms of assorted roses gracing every corner. The soft glow of twinkling fairy lights danced around us, casting a romantic ambiance upon the scene. As we exchanged vows, the gentle rustle of leaves in the breeze seemed to echo the whispered promises of forever. The intimate gathering surrounding us was deeply moved, their hearts stirred to tears by the profound significance of the moment.

When God created Adam, he was alone and took care of Eden by himself. God felt that Adam needed something and said, "It is not good for the man to be alone. I will make a helper suitable for him" (Genesis 2:18). God was playing matchmaker; He made the woman and brought her to Adam. There was nothing Adam could do about it. Adam didn't know what his needs were. There was no such thing as a woman, so he couldn't imagine one. He named many animals and spent time with them, but they did not satisfy him. There was an unfulfilled need in Adam's heart, but he didn't know what it was.

God's infinite wisdom comprehended the intricacies of Adam's soul, recognizing the profound yearning within him. He bestowed upon Adam a gift that transcended mere material desires, a gift Adam had not dared to ask for or even envision. This divine act serves as a testament to God's intimate understanding of our innermost needs, demonstrating His unfathomable love and care for His creation.

Adam exclaimed with joy because of what he had never imagined, but what he so desperately needed, when he met Eve. Adam said to Eve, who was standing before him, "This is now bone of my bones and flesh of my flesh" (Genesis 2:23). Adam had finally found happiness and contentment.

As the omniscient Creator, God perceives every facet of our existence, discerning not only our spoken requests but also the silent longings of our hearts. He meticulously crafts solutions tailored to address our deepest yearnings, orchestrating events and blessings with divine precision.

In His boundless compassion, God anticipates our needs before we even recognize them ourselves, tenderly guiding us toward fulfillment and contentment. Through His providence, He ensures that we receive exactly what is necessary for our spiritual growth and well-being, nurturing us with unwavering love and grace.

Marriage is a command from God, a sacred bond ordained by God, and holds profound significance in the journey of faith. Reflecting on Jesus' teachings, I perceive marriage as a divine invitation to embark on a spiritual pilgrimage together, with our hearts united in devotion to God.

In the sanctity of marriage, we are called to view each other as companions on this sacred journey, walking hand in hand toward the divine. It is a journey built on the pillar of trust, where we entrust our hearts to one another, and nurture a love that thrives on open and honest communication.

Within the sacred covenant of marriage, we are tasked with cherishing and respecting one another, recognizing the inherent dignity and worth bestowed upon the other by our Creator. It is a journey that requires patience as we navigate the trials and tribulations of life with steadfast perseverance.

Yet, amidst the challenges, we strive for mutual understanding, seeking to empathize with each other's perspectives and experiences. Together, our journey embodies the very essence of God's creation, where human beings are embraced as beloved children of the Divine.

The Veil of Soul

In the tender embrace of marriage, we find solace and strength, knowing that our union is blessed by God's grace. It is a journey marked by love, forgiveness, and unwavering faith, where we discover the true beauty of companionship as God intended it to be.

Chapter 7

Holy Spirit

Fate

WHILE ATTENDING COLLEGE, I joined a mountaineering club, and during a week-long winter hike with my schoolmates, as we ascended a steep mountain path, I took a moment to rest. My breath turned into vapor in the subzero air, enveloping my vision, while fleeting thoughts brushed past with the icy, piercing breeze against my right cheek.

Not long ago, at a gathering of the campus club, a friend from the mountaineering group burst into the room with an excited grin, unable to contain himself. "Have you heard? We're planning to climb that infamous mountain next week!" he exclaimed. My nearby friends, breaking the silence, began to sparkle with excitement, as if they were hearing the start of Beethoven's Symphony No. 5, "Fate."

That friend continued to explain the information he had heard with sparkling eyes, and joining the mountaineering trips with my school friends at that time was truly a delightful part of my school days, which included weekends. Arriving home after school, the first thing I did was meticulously note down the date, departure time, and necessary preparations in my monthly planner, which brought a feeling akin to walking on soft clouds. Attending church every Sunday was already a part of my past, a ritual that seemed to fade further into the recesses of my mind with each passing week. It has been so long ago, the memories of pews and hymnals growing dimmer with time, like pages yellowing in an old book left forgotten on a dusty shelf. As I continued to enjoy weekend mountain trips with my friends, the previous sense of inspiration from the Holy Spirit gradually began to fade.

Sitting on a rock, I gazed at the sky, noticing my slouched shoulders and dangling arms. "It feels like the Holy Spirit has left my side," I murmured to myself. So, amidst the mountain trails, I found myself contemplating as I ascended the rugged slopes.

According to a certain pastor's explanation, it is said that the Spirit never leaves true believers. This fact is explained in various places in the New Testament, such as Romans 8:9: "Anyone who does not have the Spirit of Christ does not belong to him." This verse clearly states that anyone whom the Spirit does not indwell is not a saved person. Therefore, if the Spirit were to depart from any believer, that person would lose their salvation relationship with Christ.

However, this contradicts the biblical teaching of the eternal assurance of believers. Another passage referring to the Spirit's permanent indwelling in the life of a believer is John 14:16, where Jesus promises that when the Father sends another Advocate, He "will be with you forever."

Furthermore, the fact that the Holy Spirit will never leave believers is confirmed in Ephesians 1:13–14: "And you also were included in Christ when you heard the message of truth, the gospel of your salvation. When you believed, you were marked in him with a seal, the promised Holy Spirit, who is a deposit guaranteeing our inheritance until the redemption of those who are God's possession—to the praise of his glory."

Trinity

God has promised eternal life to all who believe in Christ, and as a guarantee of that promise until the day of redemption, He has sent the Spirit to dwell within believers.

The reason for Christ's death, resurrection, and ascension is to send the Spirit. As Jesus promised, "But, you will receive power when the Holy Spirit comes on you; and you will be my witnesses in Jerusalem, and in all Judea and Samaria, and to the ends of the earth" (Acts 1:8).

In order for the Holy Spirit to come upon our church, Jesus had to ascend to heaven first. Beginning with Pentecost, the Spirit began to dwell permanently with believers. The eternal presence of the Spirit fulfills God's promise to never leave us and to always be with us.

While the Spirit never leaves believers, it is possible for our sin to "quench the Spirit" or "grieve the Holy Spirit," as stated in Ephesians 4:30: "And do not grieve the Holy Spirit of God, with whom you were sealed for the day of redemption." Therefore, anyone can prioritize activities such as mountaineering over God, causing their relationship with God to suffer, and without realizing it, many find themselves on the wide path, torn between the wide and narrow roads, always struggling and ultimately choosing the broad path that many people take.

Our relationship with God is secure in Christ, but unconfessed sin in our lives can hinder our fellowship with God and effectively quench the work of the Spirit in our lives. Therefore, confessing our sins is important. God is faithful and just to forgive us our sins and to cleanse us from all unrighteousness. Thus, while the Spirit never leaves us, the benefits and joy resulting from His presence can practically depart from us due to His restraint.

The moment we become Christians by believing in Jesus and confessing Him as our Savior, the Holy Spirit enters us. Although we cannot see the Spirit within ourselves with our own eyes, we can feel His presence.

Jesus mentioned about His departure from the earth, "But very truly I tell you, it is for your good that I am going away. Unless I go away, the Advocate will not come to you; but if I go, I will send him to you" (John 16:7).

Furthermore, before His Second Coming, Jesus promised to send the Holy Spirit to fill the void and described in detail the situation at His ascension when He will descend again. This assures us that His ascension was not the end but rather a promise of His return, known as the Second Coming.

> After he said this, he was taken up before their very eyes, and a cloud hid him from their sight. They were looking intently up into the sky as he was going, when suddenly two men dressed in white stood beside them. "Men of Galilee," they said, "why do you stand here looking into the sky? This same Jesus, who has been taken from you into heaven, will come back in the same way you have seen him go into heaven." (Acts 1:9–11)

We often live our lives forgetting or not being conscious of the Holy Spirit, given to us as a gift. These verses command, "Follow the Holy Spirit." This command is crucial for missionaries, pastors, local leaders, and all believers. Our Lord Jesus, filled with the Spirit, began His ministry, worked in the power of the Spirit, and walked in obedience to the Holy Spirit throughout His life. The secret to the apostles in the book of Acts becoming witnesses of the gospel, expanding the kingdom of God throughout the world with excitement, anticipation, joy, and freedom, was receiving the fullness of the Holy Spirit and following the Spirit.

His Spirit Who Lives in You

How does the Bible testify about the Holy Spirit? He is described as an eternal being, existing independently, omnipotent and omnipresent. Who is this being? Only the Creator God is the Holy Spirit.

In Matthew 28:19 Jesus states, "Therefore go and make disciples of all nations, baptizing them in the name of the Father and of the Son and of the Holy Spirit." How does Jesus start the Great Commission, the command He gave to His disciples? This means that our God is the triune God who exists as the Father, Son, and Holy Spirit, three distinct persons in one eternal, the Trinity. The Bible also testifies that the Holy Spirit possesses intellect, emotions, and will: "these are the things God has revealed to us by his Spirit. The Spirit searches all things, even the deep things of God" (1 Corinthians 2:10).

Some believers view the Holy Spirit merely as a tool to achieve their noble purposes. However, the Holy Spirit is not a means or instrument to accomplish our goals. Others perceive the Holy Spirit as an abstract concept, believing that He cannot intervene in our lives since He cannot be seen or touched. Yet, the Holy Spirit is not an abstract notion; He is the living, tangible third person of the Trinity. He is the true God who actively engages in creation and redemption, deserving of our perpetual worship, praise, and glory. As the master and architect of our lives, existence, and history, we must humbly declare, "Use me! do Your will God!"

First Corinthians 12:3 says, "Therefore I want you to know that no one who is speaking by the Spirit of God says, 'Jesus be cursed,' and no one can say, 'Jesus is Lord,' except by the Holy Spirit." This means that for someone to receive and confess Jesus as their Savior and Lord, it is only possible through the work of the Holy Spirit, and this is the baptism of the Spirit. Through this work, recorded in the Scriptures by the inspiration of the Holy Spirit, the Spirit begins to dwell within a person, as stated in Romans 8:11: "And if the Spirit of him who raised Jesus from the dead is living in you, he who raised Christ from the dead will also give life to your mortal bodies because of his Spirit who lives in you." The Bible present-tense "is living" emphasizes that the Spirit continuously resides within believers and the community of Christ, perpetually active and enduring.

The almighty and living Spirit of God comes to dwell within each of us, within our community, always ready to help us in any situation. He desires to converse with us and supply our needs. When we need wisdom, love for our daily living, and even in situations where all seems blocked and no hope is in sight, He desires to show us the way and provide answers. How amazing is it that God comes to dwell within us, living with us all year round to eternity.

What greater marvel, what more profound blessing, could there be than this? Why does the Spirit of God, the Spirit of Jesus Christ, aspire not merely to guide us to believe in Jesus for salvation, but also to establish an eternal dwelling within each of us? It's because of His profound love for every one of us who has become a child of God, seeking intimate communion and perpetual companionship with us.

It's because He longs for the advancement of God's kingdom in this world through the body of Christ, the community of believers. The greatest expression of love from parents to their children isn't found in occasional lavish gifts, but in constant presence and companionship, isn't it? Do you truly believe that the Spirit of God resides within you always? Yet, in reality, don't you sometimes feel adrift, like you are all alone? This occurs when we fail to recognize or consciously live with the Spirit of God within us, or when we neglect communion with Him.

The Spirit delves into our hearts and minds, interceding for us in alignment with God's divine purpose. Moreover, the Spirit illuminates the Scriptures to reveal their secrets to us and brings to remembrance what we have learned, guiding us into all truth.

Be Filled with the Holy Spirit

A command that the Lord gives to all believers regarding the Holy Spirit is found in Ephesians 5:18. It says, "Do not get drunk on wine, which leads to debauchery. Instead, be filled with the Spirit." This verse suggests that even believers who have been filled with the Holy Spirit can succumb to drunkenness and indulge in debauchery. Our human frailty leaves us vulnerable, and evil spirits are like roaring lions, eager to devour us. Without being filled with the Spirit, we lack the strength to overcome the desires of the flesh and our habitual sins.

In other words, we cannot become like Jesus in character if we are not resisting the temptations and attacks of evil spirits, bear fruit as witnesses of Jesus, or live as true believers who love God and love our neighbors. Therefore, "be filled with the Spirit alone" is not just a recommendation but an absolute command from the Lord to all believers. What does it mean to be filled with the Spirit? Being filled with the Spirit means being under His control. It means being in a state where the Holy Spirit fills us, rules over us, and overflows from within us.

How can we be filled with the Spirit? Being filled with the Spirit is solely a gift from God. What we need to do is to prepare ourselves to receive the filling of the Spirit. Does the Bible say that God gives the filling of the Spirit to anyone? No, it is to those who repent, as stated in Acts 2:38: "Peter replied, 'Repent and be baptized, every one of you, in the name of Jesus Christ for the forgiveness of your sins. And you will receive the gift of the Holy Spirit."

What is fundamental repentance? It is changing the master of my heart. It is changing from self to Jesus, from self to the Holy Spirit. Many believers claim to have Jesus as their Lord. However, when making small or significant decisions in life, they rely on their own interests, emotions, or experiences rather than the will of the Lord. This means that their master has not changed yet.

Revelation 3:16 says, "So, because you are lukewarm—neither hot nor cold—I am about to spit you out of my mouth." If my love for God and people has waned, neither fervent nor tepid, it warrants repentance and earnest contemplation. Just as Jesus equated hatred with murder, any harbored resentment should be a cause for repentance.

In 1 Timothy 1:15, the venerable apostle Paul proclaimed, "Here is a trustworthy saying that deserves full acceptance: Christ Jesus came into the world to save sinners—of whom I am the worst." Why did Paul, renowned for his wisdom, utter such a declaration in his later years? Not because he had committed more sins, but because he had grown in self-awareness and confessed them. As I endeavor daily to deepen my understanding of God, I increasingly identify with Paul's admission. The depth and sincerity of our surrender to the Holy Spirit determine the extent to which we are filled with His presence.

Receive Power

> Let the message of Christ dwell among you richly as you teach and admonish one another with all wisdom through psalms, hymns, and songs from the Spirit, singing to God with gratitude in your hearts. (Colossians 3:16)

It is stated that those who are filled with the Word of God in their hearts will also receive the filling of the Holy Spirit. Therefore, it is important to always read and meditate on the Scriptures.

Regarding the filling of the Spirit, 1 Thessalonians 5:19 says, "Do not quench the Spirit." This means not to extinguish the fire of the Spirit burning within us. Doubt, unbelief, pride, and impure sins extinguish the fire of the Spirit. Whether individually or as a community, when the flesh is revived, the fire of the Spirit is extinguished. Extinguishing the fire of the Holy Spirit is like kicking the Holy Spirit out of the chambers of our hearts and taking back control of our world.

The nature of the Holy Spirit is exceedingly gentle, humble, and intimate. He does not impose Himself forcefully. From my own encounters, His words are solemn, direct, yet tender. Initially, I may not grasp their full meaning, but as time unfolds and events transpire in my life, it becomes evident that those were indeed the promptings of the Holy Spirit. In essence, time unveils their truth. Consequently, when resistance in the form of doubt and impurity drives the Holy Spirit away, relegating Him to the sidelines, it evokes sighs and sadness, rendering Him unable to intervene on my behalf.

Why does our Father God desire to give us the filling of the Spirit, and what are the results? It's because when filled with the Spirit, we receive power, as stated in Acts 1:8: "But you will receive power when the Holy Spirit comes on you; and you will be my witnesses in Jerusalem, and in all Judea and Samaria, and to the ends of the earth."

What is the power given by the Holy Spirit? It's the power manifested when filled with the Holy Spirit. It includes courage to overcome even the fear of death, wisdom to oppose and defeat Satan, gentleness of heart to embrace all people, the ability to pray for others, love that embraces everyone, forgiveness, the ability to face the impossible, and the power to heal the sick, among others. By giving us this power, God enables us to become witnesses of Jesus to the ends of the earth, playing key roles in the expansion of God's kingdom.

When filled with the Spirit, we do not fulfill the desires of the flesh.

> So, I say, walk by the Spirit, and you will not gratify the desires of the flesh. For the flesh desires what is contrary to the Spirit, and the Spirit what is contrary to the flesh. They are in conflict with each other, so that you are not to do whatever you want. But if you are led by the Spirit, you are not under the law. The acts of the flesh are obvious: sexual immorality, impurity, debauchery, idolatry, and witchcraft; hatred, discord, jealousy, fits of rage, selfish ambition, dissensions, factions, and envy; drunkenness, orgies, and the like. I warn you, as I did before, that those who live like this will not inherit the kingdom of God. (Galatians 5:16–21)

Now, when we receive the Holy Spirit, there is a sense of excitement as if a new person has come, and the heart feels light as a feather, as if walking on clouds. However, after a few months, as time passes, gradually being covered by the sins of the world, the sins of the heart, one falls little by little. When this cycle repeats, stubborn sins develop. The reason for this is that although one may have repented through the work of the Holy Spirit, afterward, without being filled with the Holy Spirit, receiving the control of the Spirit. It is impossible to change one's nature through one's will and determination alone.

Romans 8:13 states, "For if you live according to the flesh, you will die; but if by the Spirit you put to death the misdeeds of the body, you will live." When filled with the Spirit, we are empowered to produce and bear beautiful and extraordinary fruit.

Galatians 5:22–23 says, "But the fruit of the Spirit is love, joy, peace, forbearance, kindness, goodness, faithfulness, gentleness, and self-control. Against such things there is no law." These fruits are the characteristics of Christ, and God's ultimate purpose for us is not only to be born again but also to become like His Son, Jesus Christ. It means thinking, speaking, and acting like Jesus. When filled with the Spirit, we can grow into mature Christians with the character of Jesus, becoming salt and light in the world, bringing about transformation wherever we are.

Overflowing with Joy

Living by the Holy Spirit is not a one-time event. If the Holy Spirit fills us every day, and even every moment, guiding and directing us, we will live a life overflowing with joy, excitement, and anticipation of blessings.

What does the Bible command us to do after we are filled with the Holy Spirit? Galatians 5:16: "But I say, walk by the Spirit, and you will not gratify the desires of the flesh." And Galatians 5:25 says, "If we live by the Spirit, let us also keep in step with the Spirit." It means to keep our pace in sync with the Spirit's pace, to follow the steps of the Spirit continually.

Furthermore, living by the Spirit means lifting our hands toward heaven, holding the flag of surrender high, and wholly relying on the Spirit, surrendering sovereignty to Him. Living under the teaching, guidance, and governance of the Spirit is indeed paramount. Failure to do so relegates us to a servant-like existence, akin to the older son in the Parable of the Prodigal Son. However, when we embrace the Spirit's leading, we inherit the privileges of God's children and align ourselves with His divine will. In essence, the Christian life boils down to one thing: living by the Spirit.

How can we receive the guidance of the Holy Spirit? By having intimate fellowship with the Holy Spirit, God shares His deep communion with the Spirit, receiving His assistance, and experiencing victory in our daily lives.

Second Corinthians 13:13 says, "The grace of the Lord Jesus Christ and the love of God and the fellowship of the Holy Spirit be with you all." "Fellowship of the Holy Spirit" means mutual interaction and communion. As our fellowship with the Holy Spirit deepens, we live by the Spirit and receive more of the spiritual blessings poured out by God. Those who deeply commune with the Spirit can communicate well with others, having been emptied and humbled. They can love God and love their neighbors.

We can share our state and seek His help and guidance in humility. Sometimes, feelings of anxiety, worry, frustration, impatience, or loneliness may flood our hearts. Suddenly, worries about the future may arise. We may set aside specific times to commune with the Holy Spirit, but we can commune with Him at any time, working, doing the house chores, and all aspects of our life.

In those moments, rather than passively accepting these emotions as unavoidable, we should openly confide in the Holy Spirit and release them. In return, the Holy Spirit fills us with heavenly peace, instills hope, and bestows fresh strength. Living under the guidance of the Holy Spirit infuses our lives with dynamism and vibrancy. We undergo fundamental changes within ourselves and eagerly await the Holy Spirit's work in our lives and in the world.

This is a life brimming with joy and happiness. When we embrace the fullness of the Holy Spirit and His guidance every moment, it's akin to having an inexhaustible power source within us. Even in the solitude of the dark tomb or cave, we can tap into this divine energy, rejuvenating our spirits and thriving victoriously.

We surrender every aspect of our lives, including the outcomes, to the Holy Spirit, and our hope knows no bounds. The undeniable truth is that within the Holy Spirit, our lives flourish with boundless freedom and happiness. Simultaneously, we embrace each challenge with renewed vigor, overcoming them with grace.

Blasphemy against the Holy Spirit

Starting with the conclusion first on this matter, "blasphemy against the Holy Spirit' encompasses any action or speech that obstructs the work of God!

Once I confided in a Christian friend, "The challenge that troubled me has been gracefully resolved through God's intervention." To my surprise, my friend wore a skeptical expression and retorted, "And? As the proverb goes, 'If you wear it on your nose, it's a nose ring; if you wear wit in your ear, it's an earring." I replied with unexpected eyes, "No need for rudeness."

Do you believe such a conversation aligns with Christian values? The concept of blasphemy against the Spirit is referenced in Mark 3:22–30 and Matthew 12:22–32. In these passages, people brought a man possessed by demons to Jesus, who healed the man of his blindness and muteness while casting out the demons. Witnessing this event led many to question if Jesus was indeed the Savior they had long awaited. "All the people were astonished and said, "Could this be the Son of David?" (Matthew 12:23).

After hearing stories about the Messiah, a group of Pharisees quickly attempted to quell the budding faith emerging within the crowd. They spoke in order to swiftly cut off the budding leaves of belief. "But when the Pharisees heard this, they said, "It is only by Beelzebul, the prince of demons, that this fellow drives out demons" (Matthew 12:24).

I can't fathom Jesus's frustration upon hearing such disrespectful remarks. He spoke about blasphemy against the Holy Spirit and presented several arguments to refute the Pharisees' claim that he cast out demons by the power of Satan: "And so I tell you, every kind of sin and slander can be forgiven, but blasphemy against the Spirit will not be forgiven. Anyone who speaks a word against the Son of Man will be forgiven, but anyone who speaks against the Holy Spirit will not be forgiven, either in this age or in the age to come" (Matthew 12:31–32).

Blasphemy against the Spirit is related to condemning Jesus Christ as being filled with evil spirits rather than the Holy Spirit.

In my opinion, even today any human accused with this kind a comment will not be acceptable. This particular type of blasphemy cannot be repeated today. The Pharisees had a unique moment in history. They had the Law and the Prophets, the Spirit moving their hearts, the Son of God standing before them, and they witnessed the miracles He performed with their own eyes. Never in history has there been such a profound revelation of divine light to humanity as at that moment.

If there were ever people who should have recognized who Jesus was, it should have been the intelligent Pharisees, who demonstrated thoroughness in adhering to the letter of the Law and upheld the traditions of Jewish theology. However, they chose resistance. Despite knowing the truth and having evidence, they deliberately attributed the work of the Holy Spirit to the work of Satan. Jesus declared their obstinate blindness to be an unforgivable sin. Their blasphemy against the Holy Spirit, resisting the Spirit, signifies their ultimate rejection of God's grace. They chose their path, and God did not prevent them from heading toward destruction.

Jesus told the crowd that the Pharisees' blasphemy against the Holy Spirit meant they would not receive forgiveness in this age or in the age to come. This was another way of expressing that their sin is unforgivable. Blasphemy against the Holy Spirit is a sin that remains unforgiven now and forever, a sin that will not be forgiven. Why is it an eternal sin? Simply put, because the one they sinned against is eternal, the Alpha and the Omega, the beginning and the end, God Himself. Therefore, they committed an eternal sin against the Eternal One, and we too can commit such an unforgivable eternal sin.

The Pharisees' public rejection of Christ and God immediately manifested in the following chapter. Jesus began speaking to them in parables for the first time. The disciples were bewildered by this change in Jesus' teaching method, and Jesus explained why He was using parables:

> He replied, "Because the knowledge of the secrets of
> the kingdom of heaven has been given to you, but not

to them. Whoever has will be given more, and they will have an abundance. Whoever does not have, even what they have will be taken from them. This is why I speak to them in parables: 'Though seeing, they do not see; though hearing, they do not hear or understand.'" (Matthew 13:11–13)

Once again, the sin of blaspheming the Holy Spirit should not be repeated by anyone today, no matter how tempted. Christ is not on this earth; He sits at the right hand of God. No one can personally witness Jesus performing miracles or attribute His power to anyone other than the Spirit.

The unforgivable sin in today's terms is a persistent state of disbelief. The Holy Spirit rebukes the world concerning sin, righteousness, and judgment. To persist in rebellion against this rebuke and deliberately refuse to repent is to blaspheme the Spirit. Anyone who rejects the Spirit urging them to believe in Jesus Christ and dies in unbelief will have no forgiveness of sins in this world or the world to come.

God's love is undoubtfully, most definitely clear! As Jesus states in John 3:16, "For God so loved the world that he gave his one and only Son, that whoever believes in him shall not perish but have eternal life."

The choice is clear, and the selection is also evident, as Jesus states in John 3:36: "Whoever believes in the Son has eternal life, but whoever rejects the Son will not see life, for God's wrath remains on them."

The longsuffering patience of God, who waits for us, is described in Mathew 12:20–21: "A bruised reed he will not break, and a smoldering wick he will not snuff out, till he has brought justice through to victory. In his name the nations will put their hope."

Chapter 8

Easter

All the Meaning

CHRISTIANITY DIFFERS FROM OTHER religions in several keyways. The most important is the Jesus's physical resurrection apart as it focuses on victory over death. Christianity revolves around the belief that Jesus Christ is the Son of God, fully divine and fully human, who came to save humanity through His death and resurrection. This is distinct from other faiths, where leaders are often viewed as prophets or wise teachers, not divine saviors. What is resurrection? Resurrection, a term frequently mentioned in the Bible, primarily signifies the event of Jesus rising from the dead three days following his crucifixion. It marks a pivotal moment, signifying not only Jesus's triumph over death but also the promise of believers being resurrected upon their death through their faith in Jesus. In John 6:44, Jesus says, "No one can come to me unless the father who sent me draws them, and I will raise them up at the last day." Resurrection is when a person dies and comes back to life.

As stated in John 20:19, "On the evening of that first day of the week, when the disciples were together, with the doors locked in fear of the Jewish leaders, Jesus came and stood among them and said, 'Peace be with you!'"After Jesus rose from death on the cross, the disciples were trembling with fear. Jesus proclaimed when He appeared to them. What He wanted to give them was true peace.

As a testament to the restoration, He proclaimed peace, the peace of heaven, which was not just for the disciples, but for the many who were still suffering in the darkness of sin. The kingdom of God that Jesus proclaimed is righteousness, peace, and joy in the Holy Spirit. His resurrection brought peace and joy to the disciples. Jesus, who rose from the dead, knows that the greatest fear of all human beings is death. The tremor-inducing grip of emotions seizes every human soul when confronted with the unknown and the unexpected. Among these tumultuous experiences, the specter of death looms largest, sending shivers down the spine and casting a shadow over the heart. Yet, a life shackled by the relentless fear of mortality can never bask in the tranquil embrace of peace and the radiant glow of joy.

First Birth of Eternal Life

Death is the final event of leaving this world, but it is also the first birth event of eternal life given by Jesus's death on the cross. We speculates that Jesus' words to Thomas made it clear to each person that the resurrected Jesus was the same Jesus who had been among people for three and a half years at that time, and Jesus had been crucified, passed through the valley of death, and resurrected. Each aspect of Jesus had not changed in the slightest, although Jesus' body was marked with nail marks.

At the same time, Jesus also let people know that he had come down from the cross, overcome sin, overcome suffering, and overcome death, that his nail marks were evidence of his victory over Satan, that he had become a sin offering and successfully redeemed the whole human race, and that he had already taken on the sins of mankind and completed his work.

For the believer in the resurrection, death is no longer a fear. We should not be troubled in our hearts, but rejoice and live our life joyfully in the acknowledgement that the risen Lord, our

Savior, is eternal peace. Human efforts to accomplish peace are futile; however, we as believers receive eternal peace when the Holy Spirit indwells in our heart. And with that we as believers in Christ continuously long for his connection to our God.

Jesus' resurrection means that he will never die again and will live forever in his resurrection body, making him the first fruits of the resurrection. Now let's look for some Bible verses that relate to resurrection prophecies.

Let's look at the Mathew 16:1, where the Pharisees and Sadducees came to test Jesus and asked him to show them a miracle from heaven. These two groups are often mentioned in the Bible and are constantly at odds with each other, testing Jesus.

The Sadducees and Pharisees made up the ruling class of Israel. While there are many similarities between the two groups, there are also important differences. Both groups followed the Law of Moses and had political power. The Sadducees were doctrinally conservative, but the Pharisees were hypocrites who elevated the Old Testament to the same level as God and dismissed as worthless anything they couldn't find in the Scriptures.

The differences between the Pharisees and Sadducees can be seen in several passages in the Bible and in the extant writings of the Pharisees. Religiously speaking, the Sadducees were more conservative in one doctrinal area: they insisted on a literal interpretation of the biblical text. The Pharisees, on the other hand, placed the oral tradition on equal authority with the written word of God.

The Sadducees refused to believe in the resurrection of the dead, but the Pharisees did. The Sadducees denied an afterlife, believing that the soul disappears at death, while the Pharisees believed in an afterlife and rewards and punishments for each individual. The Sadducees denied an invisible spiritual world, but the Pharisees taught about the existence of angels and demons in the spiritual realm.

In the Bible, the Sadducees were an aristocratic elite, and the priests and the high priest were Sadducees, so they were in a wealthier and more powerful position. The Pharisees represented the working class and were respected by them.

The Sadducees were more interested in politics than religion, so they ignored Jesus until they began to fear that he might upset the status quo by unnecessarily attracting Roman attention. It was at this point that both the Sadducees and Pharisees put aside their differences and conspired together to put Christ to death.

Back to the Bible verses, these hypocrites, who had wealth and power based solely on the Law, put Jesus to the test and demanded that he show them a miracle. Jesus, who already knew their lustful intentions, told them,

> "When evening comes, you say, 'It will be fair weather, for the sky is red,' and in the morning, 'Today it will be stormy, for the sky is red and overcast.' You know how to interpret the appearance of the sky, but you cannot interpret the signs of the times. A wicked and adulterous generation looks for a sign, but none will be given it except the sign of Jonah." Jesus then left them and went away. (Matthew 12:2-4)

Even more importantly, Jesus considered the story of Jonah to be true:"For as Jonah was three days and three nights in the belly of a huge fish, so the Son of Man will be three days and three nights in the heart of the earth" (Matthew 12:40). This means that Jesus was predicting that his death and resurrection would be like Jonah's miracle. Therefore, to deny that the story of Jonah's fish is a historical fact that actually happened would make Jesus a liar, or, even if not intentionally, would deny his divinity.

Not the Bread

Let's continue to look at the following conversation between Jesus and disciples: "'Be careful,' Jesus said to them. 'Be on your guard against the yeast of the Pharisees and Sadducees'" (Matthew 16:6). The response from the disciples: "They discussed this among themselves and said, 'It is because we didn't bring any bread'" (16:7). The disciples, in their forgetfulness about bringing bread and their guilt-ridden misunderstanding of Jesus' words, end up squabbling amongst themselves.

When Jesus notices the disciples' and their frustrating behavior, "aware of their discussion, Jesus asked, 'You of little faith, why are you talking among yourselves about having no bread?'" (16:8). Then, Jesus remined to them about the miracle of five loaves for the five thousand and the seven loaves for the four thousand, and how many basketfuls they gathered afterward. And he said, "'How is it you don't understand that I was not talking to you about bread? But be on your guard against the yeast of the Pharisees and Sadducees'" (16:11).

According to the Bible, Jesus's disciples held diverse professions. Andrew, Peter, James, and John, sons of Zebedee, earned their living as fishermen. Simon was designated as the Zealot, though it is not strictly a profession. Matthew, on the other hand, worked as a tax collector for the Roman government, displaying some level of education. The specific occupations of the other disciples remain undisclosed in the Bible. In the context of this verse, one can imagine the potential frustration Jesus, as the embodiment of God on earth, might have felt dealing with disciples of varying education levels, perhaps necessitating repeated explanations to convey his teachings effectively.

In all portraits of Jesus painted by famous artists, He is depicted with a only soft, gentle demeanor, with which some, including myself, find slight disagreement. The Bible, however, states that Jesus embodied a strong, masculine presence as a powerful leader. Here are couple of examples:

> Jesus entered the temple courts and drove out all who were buying and selling there. He overturned the tables of the money changers and the benches of those selling doves. "It is written," he said to them, 'My house will be called a house of prayer,' but you are making it 'a den of robbers." (Matthew 21:12)

And Jesus used harsh language to point out that the Pharisees' hearts were full of venom. He described the Pharisees as "children of vipers" (Matthew 12:34) and "serpents, brood of vipers" (Matthew 23:33), declaring their impending wrath and future judgment of hell punishment.

And the disciples realized what Jesus was trying to convey to them. "Then they understood that he was not telling them to guard against the yeast used in bread, but against the teaching of the Pharisees and Sadducees" (Matthew 16:12).

Who Do You Think I Am?

If we continue to read Matthew 16:13–21, we will find the verse that predicts of Jesus' death: "From that time on Jesus began to explain to his disciples that he must go to Jerusalem and suffer many things at the hands of the elders, the chief priests and the teachers of the law, and that he must be killed and on the third day be raised to life" (Matthew 16:21).

And now we look deeper into the beginning verse, Matthew 16:13. The process of leading Peter to confess his faith in the Lord unfolds through dialogue.

> When Jesus came to the region of Caesarea Philippi, he asked his disciples, "Who do people say the Son of Man is?" They replied, "Some say John the Baptist; others say Elijah; and still others, Jeremiah or one of the prophets." "But what about you?" he asked. "Who do you say I am?" (Matthew 16:13–15)

The crucial essence of the condensed scripture above lies in the necessity of a clear confession of faith and how that confession should become the centerpiece of believers' lives.

When asked, "Who do you say the Son of Man is?" Simon Peter confesses, "You are the Messiah, the Son of the living God" (Matthew 16:16). Confessing precisely who Jesus is marks the beginning of a right relationship with the Lord and a life of proper faith. Believing and confessing Jesus as the "Son of the living God" is a truth possible only through the enlightenment of the Holy Spirit. Jesus promises to build his church on the rock of faith like Peter's confession, a church against which the gates of Hades will not prevail. And Jesus said,

> "And I tell you that you are Peter, and on this rock, I will build my church, and the gates of Hades will not overcome it. I will give you the keys of the kingdom of heaven; whatever you bind on earth will be bound in heaven, and whatever you loose on earth will be loosed in heaven." Then he ordered his disciples not to tell anyone that he was the Messiah. From that time on Jesus began to explain to his disciples that he must go to Jerusalem and suffer many things at the hands of the elders, the chief priests, and the teachers of the law, and that he must be killed and on the third day be raised to life. (Matthew 16:18–21)

Observing Peter's confession of faith, we realize that our own confession must come from our lips. It should not merely be intellectual knowledge but a confession stemming from faith deep within our hearts. Receiving the keys to the kingdom of heaven from Jesus means receiving the authority to open the doors of heaven and grant access to those assured of salvation. Therefore, those who believe receive this astonishing and unbelievable authority—the keys to the kingdom—and should use the binding and losing power given by the Lord to bind the forces of Satan daily and to release those bound, becoming channels of blessing. Imagine the immense spiritual authority, unseen to the eye, capable of capturing the forces of Satan—it's a remarkable spiritual weapon.

The decisive reason Peter received the keys to the kingdom of heaven is because he realized and confessed that Jesus is the Messiah. The keys to the kingdom are given to those who recognize Jesus as the Messiah.

Peter's faith, in recognizing Christ in this way, is a great blessing worthy of receiving the keys to the kingdom. However, the Bible says that Christ has been a secret of God hidden from the ages.

The reason Jesus said Peter is blessed is because his confession is not of his own flesh. Peter's confession was revealed by God the Father. Peter's correct confession of faith was not from his own ability but from God, and that's why it came forth.

Furthermore, Throughout the Bible, one encounters numerous passages elucidating the resurrection of Jesus, often imparting understanding to His disciples and a multitude of other individuals.

> "The Son of Man must be delivered over to the hands of sinners, be crucified and on the third day be raised again." (Luke 24:7)

> Jesus said to her, "I am the resurrection and the life. The one who believes in me will live, even though they die." (John 11:25)

> "Before long, the world will not see me anymore, but you will see me. Because I live, you also will live." (John 14:19)

> "But God raised him from the dead, freeing him from the agony of death, because it was impossible for death to keep its hold on him." (Acts 2:24)

> "For he has set a day when he will judge the world with justice by the man he has appointed. He has given proof of this to everyone by raising him from the dead." (Acts 17:31)

> And if Christ has not been raised, your faith is futile; you are still in your sins. (1 Corinthians 15:17)

> Remember Jesus Christ, raised from the dead, descended from David. This is my gospel. (2 Timothy 2:8)

While pondering over these verses, can we truly grasp the profound depths of God's love, which flows through our hearts and pulses through our veins?—"Because I live, you also will live."

In conclusion, it is with profound gratitude that we acknowledge how God meticulously selected and ordained each of us from our mother's womb, purposefully sending us into this world. Our hearts overflow with reverence as we reflect on the sacrifice of our Lord Jesus Christ, who willingly endured three agonizing days in the sin of our tomb to atone for our sins and rose from the dead. Why did Jesus undertake such a monumental act of love on my behalf? It was out of an unfathomable depth of compassion, a divine desire to bestow upon us the gift of eternal life. He, the exalted Son of God, relinquished the splendor of heaven to walk among us in the lowliest form of humanity, all for the sake of our redemption.

In the wake of Jesus' death and resurrection, He stands not only as the pinnacle of deity but also as the King of kings. His victory over death transcends comprehension, serving as the ultimate beacon of hope in a world fraught with uncertainty. Therefore, let us live out our days in reverent adoration, glorifying His name with every breath we take until the time comes for us to return to our heavenly home, our souls forever glorified with His divine grace.

Chapter 9

The Future

Unknown Future

ONE SUNNY DAY IN the past, as the radiant sun illuminated our path, my friends and I leisurely strolled through a bustling shopping center. Ahead, a cluster of people congregated in front of a television set within an electronics store. Their voices filled the air with urgency, drawings my curiosity.

Intrigued, I made my way closer, joining the group silently as we all fixed our gaze on the screen. The unfolding spectacle held us captive, eliciting a mix of emotions. Amidst the chaos, a mournful shout escaped my lips.

This moment occurred during my visit to the US Virgin Islands, embarking on a two-week vacation to reconnect with a friend. The television broadcasted the harrowing events of September 11, 2001—a day etched in history for its tragic hijackings. The shaky voice of the news anchor delivered the grim updates, recounting the plane's collision with the iconic Twin Towers.

The day before the tragedy unfolded, I had arrived there via Newark Airport, just sixteen miles from One World Trade Center, where the Twin Towers were located. Goosebumps prickled my skin at the mere thought of what could have been had if I had flown just a day later to reach the islands.

Upon witnessing the broadcast, I immediately reached out to my travel agency, desperate to inquire about returning flights. However, all flights to the mainland were suspended, leaving me stranded on the serene island, uncertain of what the future held. I grappled with the unknown, trying to find solace amidst the bittersweet beauty of the tropical paradise that surrounded me. Each glance towards the St. Thomas beach horizon filled me with a mixture of awe and apprehension.

Despite the lingering shadow of the tragic incident, I endeavored to immerse myself in the island's wonders. I embarked on scenic drives through lush mountainsides, delved into the rich history for Christian, and wandered the vibrant streets adorned with colonial architecture. Yet, the specter of the recent evets lingered in the back burner of my brain, a startling reminder of the fragility of life.

It wasn't until ten days later, when my travel agent reached out with a news of a rebooked flight routing through Puerto Rico, that I found a way back to the mainland. With a mix of relief and trepidation, I held back the surge of emotions stirred by situation, and I journeyed back to the United States, finally returning to Seattle.

The vivid memory of that illustration above reminds me that had I known what lay ahead during that period of time, I wouldn't have eagerly planned that once-in-a-lifetime trip to such a magnificent destination. It's sharply defined that we are often denied or cannot comprehend the unraveling events coming from the future.

Let's look into how the Bible explains that we do not know the future: "Since no one knows the future, who can tell someone else what is to come?" (Ecclesiastes 8:7). "When times are good, be happy; but when times are bad, consider this: God has made the one as well as the other. Therefore, no one can discover anything about their future" (Ecclesiastes 7:14). In the Bible verses above, we assume that when something good and happy occurs, we automatically think it will always be good and happy and if, when something sad or bad happens, it will always stay that way, that's why God sometimes gives us joy and sometimes gives us hardship. That's why we should never try to predict the future. Some people still visit fortune tellers and pay hefty sums in hopes of learning about their future. But God tells us to ask God about everything that will happen in the future, because all the future is in the hands of God, the almighty Creator.

Therefore, a philosopher once said, "Do not rejoice too much, nor grieve too much," because in time you realize that what you rejoiced over was not so worth rejoicing, and what you grieved over was not so grievous. Therefore, the interpretation is that we don't know the future, which is to say, we don't know the passage of time in our own lives.

Control of Your Future

Let's look at another prospective about control of your future. As we heard many times in the past, if we get a great education it will guarantee for bright future. A lot of colleges or universities try to lure students to attend with their heartfelt brochures saying things like, "Take control of your future! Do you feel excited about your career? Many of us expect our organizations and leaders to manage our career and our learning and development and to provide us with the right opportunities your future . . . ," etc.

Certainly! And I absolutely agree wholeheartedly that everyone, regardless of their financial situation, should have access to quality education and be able to meet the requirements set forth by schools. It's essential that individuals have the opportunity to pursue their educational aspirations without any hindrances.

What about financial security? As we all know and hear about it all the time, financial security refers to the ability to afford your expenses, live comfortably on your income, and save for the future. It means having enough savings to cover yourself when times are tough. Therefore, we look into right investments, saving, stocks, bonds, mutual funds, exchange-traded funds, options, futures, derivatives, and foreign exchange, etc.

Are education and financial security the only things we need for our bright future?

Of course, we cannot forget to go to the gym, exercise, and eat right! What else?

Have you ever pondered the utter dedication we humans invest in upkeeping our physical being? It's like we're all in a never-ending cable subscription service for body maintenance, complete with daily workouts and menu updates for following days!

On the journey of life, no one can predict what lies ahead, not even a minute or a second into the future. There are moments when events unfold before our eyes, yet we struggle to comprehend their significance. As humans, we are bound by the uncertainty of the future, yet we continue our path with optimism, often unaware of the proximity of death. While we may believe we are in control of our destiny, life's course doesn't always align with our plans. Sometimes, we find ourselves undertaking actions without hesitation, actions that defy our common sense, knowledge, wisdom, and experience. When we witness the sorrowful and bewildering tragedies unfolding in the world, it's easy to despair for the future of humanity. However, we must remember that the history and destiny of mankind rest in the hands of a higher power.

Let's examine a few Bible verses that describe God as the creator and controller of our futures.

> It is I who made the earth and created mankind on it My own hands stretched out the heavens; I marshaled their starry hosts. I will raise up Cyrus in my righteousness; I will make all his ways straight. He will rebuild my city and set my exiles free, but not for a price of reward, says the LORD Almighty. (Isaiah 45:12–13)

He guides each step of our lives with precision: "A person's steps are directed by the LORD. How then can anyone understand their own way?" (Proverbs 20:24). Moreover, God desires us to pray and surrender all our burdens to Him, trusting that He will orchestrate our lives: "To humans belong the plans of the heart, but from the LORD comes the proper answer of the tongue . . . Commit to the

LORD whatever you do, and he will establish your plans" (Proverbs 16:1, 3).

Reassuring Guidance

The Bible teaches us that as we reflect on our lives and contemplate the future, the deeds of the righteous and the wise are entrusted to God's care. Whether we will embrace or despise what lies ahead remains unknown to us. Yet, it is evident that individuals from all walks of life—the righteous and the wicked, the virtuous and the flawed, the pure and the impure, the faithful and the sinful, those who embrace sacrifice and those who reject it—share a common destiny. Therefore, we find guidance on how to navigate life by entrusting everything to God's providence.

> Go, eat your food with gladness, and drink your wine with a joyful heart, for God has already approved what you do. Always be clothed in white, and always anoint your head with oil. Enjoy life with your wife, whom you love, all the days of this meaningless life that God has given you under the sun—all your meaningless days. For this is your lot in life and in your toilsome labor under the sun. Whatever your hand finds to do, do it with all you might, for in the realm of the dead, where you are going, there is neither working nor planning nor knowledge nor wisdom. (Ecclesiastes 9:7–10)

Therefore, it's imperative to gain a clear understanding of our Heavenly Father's nature and to assess our current circumstances. This awareness empowers us, the chosen ones, to face the future without fear. While the concept may seem straightforward, translating it into action can be challenging. It requires a conscious decision to confront our reality head-on, to lay everything out before us, and to move forward with purpose and resolve.

As most of us were when we were growing up, navigating the unfamiliar terrain of school and grappling with new challenges often filled us with hesitation and fear. In those moments, we found solace and guidance in our parents' wisdom. Whether it was the first day of kindergarten, facing a daunting math test, or summoning the courage to join the soccer team, their reassuring words were like a beacon in the storm of uncertainty. With a gentle smile and a reassuring pat on the back, they instilled in us the confidence to tackle whatever obstacles lay ahead.

If we truly believe in God, what reason do we have to fear when our Heavenly Father assures us that He is in charge of our future? If we find ourselves apprehensive about what lies ahead, feeling as though we're stumbling through the dense fog of a murky morning with heavy, damp air weighing us down, we should turn to prayer. In our prayers, we can beseech God for guidance, seeking His enlightenment and wisdom to illuminate our path.

As children of God, we should find joy in the abundant blessings bestowed upon us, even now, at the banquet of our Heavenly Father, who reigns over the entire universe and all its wonders. God has granted us the mandate to be fruitful and multiply, to replenish the earth, and to exercise stewardship over it, and we should delight in these gifts with order and moderation. God's desire for His children is for us to rejoice always, to maintain a constant communion with Him through prayer, and to express gratitude in all circumstances.

Here is our Father God, gently guides us, instructing us in the ways to be happy in the Bible: "Rejoyce always, pray continually, give thanks in all circumstances; for this is God's will for you in Christ Jesus" (1 Thessalonians 5:16–18). And he encourages us, "Rejoice in the Lord always; again, I will say, rejoice" (Philippians 4:4). Joy, peace and happiness are privilege of Childrens of God. He remembers and keeps what he has promised: "He provides food for those who fear him; he remembers his covenant forever" (Psalm 111: 5).

In our lives, there will always be incidents that happen unexpectedly, causing worries and fears. However, in those seemingly inevitable circumstances, we must hold onto His hand and continue walking along the life path that unfolds before us, buoyed by the invisible carrier of God's grace. Instead of complaining about the challenges we face, let us trust that they will be smoothed out in ways of tremendous wisdom, even if those ways are presently unknown to us. Let us live our lives joyfully, singing songs of grace and offering gratitude to the Divine, who has chosen us as His children.

Near-Death Encounters

I once viewed a program showcasing several individuals' near-death encounters. Among them, a man recounted his brief testimony detailing his arrival in heaven and encountering Jesus face to face. He described witnessing his entire life, from birth to the present, unfolding like a documentary before him. He confessed that throughout many parts of this cinematic revelation, he couldn't bear to look up, overwhelmed by the embarrassment and shame of observing his own flaws and failings.

And then, there was another man who embarked on a journey strikingly similar to the first. At first, he witnessed the aftermath of his own actions, witnessing the sorrow and hurt he had inflicted upon others, whether through thoughtless words or thoughtless deeds. It was in those moments that he began to truly understand the depth of their pain, feeling it resonate within his own heart, as if he were experiencing their anguish alongside them. Then he expressed relief, finding solace in the fact that his efforts to assist others as a paramedic served as a form of redemption, offsetting the wrongs he had committed against other people.

Reflecting on his experience, I pondered my own life's panorama, considering my actions of the years of life, past month, week, yesterday, and today. Repentance welled up within me, and I earnestly prayed for the cleansing power of Jesus' blood. In a single moment, we can find ourselves culpable of sin, often without even realizing it. Maybe that's why theaa apostle Paul said in the Bible, "I crucify myself daily to the cross," as stated in Galatians 2:20: "I have been crucified with Christ and I no longer live, but Christ lives in me. The life I now live in the body, I live by faith in the Son of God, who loved me and gave himself for me."

As we all know, no one lives forever in this world without experiencing death. Our ancestors have all passed away, and we hear their stories recounted by the living through oral tradition. Death confronts everyone, regardless of their goodness or wickedness, no matter how illustrious, because God has imposed a limit on all life since Adam's sin, as stated in Psalm 90:3: "You turn people back to dust, saying, "Return to dust, you mortals."

We all desire to live happily ever after without contemplating death, but as we reach the end of our lives, lying in bed before our families, we realize our powerlessness in the face of it. In the Bible, Jesus instructs us to deny ourselves, meaning to metaphorically die to our own desires and take up our cross, and He emphasizes that those who aspire to enter heaven must repent. Only the living possesses the agency to deny themselves, while the deceased are incapable of such action.

Viewing this statement from another perspective, particularly from the standpoint of spiritual death, one cannot truly deny oneself. The spiritually dead individual lacks the capacity to deny themselves and therefore cannot genuinely repent. The ability to deny oneself is a privilege reserved for the spiritually alive alone. The dead cannot love, hate, envy, or engage in any action, particularly repentance. They are devoid of further opportunities. Let's look at a couple of Bible verses.

> But do not forget this one thing, dear friends: With the Lord a day is like a thousand years, and a thousand years are like a day. The Lord is not slow in keeping his promise, as some understand slowness. Instead, he is patient with you, not wanting anyone to perish, but everyone to come to repentance. (2 Peter 3:8–9)

> "And I'll say to myself, "You have plenty of grain laid up for many years. Take life easy; eat, drink and be merry." But God said to him, 'You fool! This very night your life will be demanded from you. Then who will get what you have prepared for yourself?'" (Luke 12:19–20)

To be alive means having numerous opportunities, unlike the dead, who have none. There's the opportunity to repent and

The Future

forgive, to perform acts of kindness. You have the chance to rejoice, to express gratitude, to pray incessantly, and to live joyfully with your loved ones. Therefore, these Bible verses teach us the way to live and serve God.

> Be very careful, then, how you live—not as unwise but as wise, making the most of every opportunity, because the days are evil." (Ephesians 5:15–16)

> And do not forget to do good and to share with others, for with such sacrifices God is pleased. (Hebrews 13:16)

> The end of all things is near. Therefore, be alert and of sober mind so that you may pray. Above all, love each other deeply, because love covers over a multitude of sins. Offer hospitality to one another without grumbling. Each of you should use whatever gift you have received to serve others, as faithful stewards of God's grace in its various forms. If anyone speaks, they should do so as one who speaks the very words of God. If anyone serves, they should do so with the strength God provides, so that in all things God may be praised through Jesus Christ. To him be the glory and the power for ever and ever. Amen. (1 Peter 4:7–11)

The fact that we are alive now signifies that we still have the chance to live righteously. Therefore, we should seize the opportunity and endeavor to shape our lives into virtuous ones. We all acknowledge that these tasks aren't grand or arduous. For no one knows when Jesus will return on the clouds with the sound of the trumpet; only God in heaven knows.

> But the day of the Lord will come like a thief. The heavens will disappear with a roar; the elements will be destroyed by fire, and the earth and everything done in it will be laid bare. Since everything will be destroyed in this way, what kind of people ought you to be? You ought to live holy and godly lives as you look forward to the day of God and speed its coming. That day will bring about the destruction of the heavens by fire, and the elements will melt in the heat. But in keeping with his promise we are

looking forward to a new heaven and a new earth, where righteousness dwells. So then, dear friends, since you are looking forward to this, make every effort to be found spotless, blameless and at peace with him. (2 Peter 3:10–14)

Don't Have to Be Special

There were two individuals in the Bible who ascended to heaven without experiencing death: Enoch and Elijah. Enoch's life is briefly noted in Genesis 5:24: "Enoch walked faithfully with God; then he was no more, because God took him away." And as stated in Hebrews 11:5, "By faith Enoch was taken from this life, so that he did not experience death: 'He could not be found, because God had taken him away.' For before he was taken, he was commended as one who pleased God." Although his remarkable life isn't extensively detailed, one notable aspect is his translation to heaven without undergoing death.

Elijah was a man of many miracles and wonders, a man of many gifts, and a prophet who was called a marvelous prophet. As mentioned in the last chapter, when Jesus asked his disciples, "Whom do people say that I am?" they replied, "Elijah," which was a great compliment in that time. Elijah was also a successful servant of God and a role model. Enoch pales in comparison, and nothing he did is recorded in the Bible. He has no leadership titles, no miracles, and no ministry, only the statement that he walked with God.

In our current generation, we often gauge greatness by outward signs, wonders, and achievements. Our emphasis on visible outcomes and markers has established the criteria for our faith's depth. Undoubtedly, Enoch and Elijah held a special place in God's favor. However, unlike Elijah, Enoch, though not widely known or esteemed as a great saint, found favor with God simply by walking in close communion with Him. A life characterized by walking in harmony with God is what truly delights Him the most. Numerous

Christian books are available, serving as guides for becoming children of God and exploring the diverse paths of discipleship.

The way to please God is very simple. It is to walk with Him, even when we feel ordinary. It involves accompanying Him daily by pondering His thoughts, conversing with Him through prayer with sincerity, envisioning His plans, and understanding His desires for us. These actions bear resemblance to expressions of human love. When one falls in love with another, they deeply care about their partners preferences, favorite foods, music tastes, and hobbies. We need not strive for greatness or historical significance to please God; we need not consider ourselves special. God's work is accomplished through individuals who walk closely with Him, not necessarily those deemed extraordinary. If you and I are considered special, it's because God sees us that way.

I would like to include the eyewitness account of my own mother passing in my book titled *Father and Father*. During my mother's final moments as she departed from this earth, the scene remained unseen by my siblings. However, my mother, with vivid clarity, described the remarkable event unfolding before her eyes. It began with my mother lying in bed, her right arm raised, reaching into the empty air as if searching for something intangible. I stood beside her, silently sharing the moment, watching her hand move gently. She was tracing the outline of a cross suspended in the air, a vision known only to her. Pointing her finger toward the hospital ceiling in astonishment, she whispered to herself: angels were descending from heaven to welcome her, their ethereal forms draped in white, serenading her with a celestial song of welcome. Her joy overflowed as she beheld them, her eyes reflecting pure happiness and wonder. And she departed from this earth to transit to the eternal happy place, heaven. She lived her ordinary life as a Christian, raising us and performing as a typical housewife.

> But seek first his kingdom and his righteousness, and all these things will be given to you as well. (Matthew 6:33)

Chapter 10

Angels

Early Life

A MONTH-OLD BABY GIRL, scarcely after her birth, abruptly ceased breastfeeding. Despite her mother's tender attempts to cradle her against her warm chest, the serene infant, resembling an angel in repose, remained deeply asleep. With eyelids veiling her gaze, the baby girl's eyes moved restlessly, as if pondering the experiences she had encountered since entering the world and the dreams she may have been weaving. Despite the mother's earnest efforts to rouse the baby, who neither nursed nor stirred from slumber, her heart swelled with a mixture of longing and sorrow. Yet, the baby girl persisted in her tranquil sleep, oblivious to her mother's silent anguish, causing the mother's heart to slowly dissolve in resignation.

After three days had passed, it became necessary to awaken the baby, who stood at the crossroads of life and death due to dehydration and malnutrition. With a fearful heart, knowing help was imperative, the mother was compelled to call for the aid of the only available medical practitioner in her rural location. By the hand of the practitioner, with his careful precision, acupuncture needles were applied to vital points, rousing the baby from her deep slumber. Finally awake, she cautiously moistened her parched throat and resumed breastfeeding, thus reclaiming her health.

The baby continued to breastfeed from her mother, yet her physical development lagged significantly. Even months later, she remained inactive unlike other children, frail and dependent like a dry branch, often lying down or leaning against walls. Though the mother herself was not malnourished, her child was wasting away, reminiscent of Ethiopian children suffering. It wasn't until later that the mother discovered she was pregnant with another child, realizing her body might have unintentionally kept necessary nutrition from her baby girl due to this revelation. Suddenly struck by inspiration, she concocted a remedy of sorts from two eels living in the well, intending to feed them to her child. After much effort, she finally managed to catch the elusive eels, hoping they would bring nourishment to her ailing child.

A variety of herbs and beneficial vegetables were added to the eels, and it took a long time to create a mixture until all the ingredients turned into liquid form. After consuming the mixture, which was thickly coated with eel oil, the child regained her appetite and began eating food again, consuming a substantial amount. Subsequently, as if the long-awaited rain had suddenly arrived during a drought, and as if a flood was imminent, the child became large but cute. She started toddling and walking around.

Additionally, throughout her upbringing, she encountered a dozen or so instances where she faced minor injuries and accidents. Yet, through some magical resilience, she was not only endured but thrived, maturing into adulthood. Her siblings observed in astonishment, silently acknowledging the trials she endured on her journey through life. Eventually, she blossomed into a woman of health intellect and beauty.

The above recounts the true events of my early life as shared with me by my mother. My journey has been marked by trials and tribulations. Despite my contemplation of the mysteries surrounding these experiences, I maintain a steadfast belief in the presence of guiding angels who encircle and protect me. It's conceivable that divine intervention led my mother to extract the eels from the well, nourishing me through times of malnutrition. Furthermore, I am convinced that my guardian angel has stood watch during every accident and incident, ensuring I emerged unscathed, spared from enduring life-altering injuries. Even after became an adult, there were many close calls that I've experience, but I've survived. These are listed in one of my other books, titled *Father and Father*.

Consider this scenario: At the age of eleven, mid-game with a friend, I choked on a snack, gasping for air in another room. My six-year-old companion, mistaking it for play, simply stood by, a curious spectator. How remarkable it was that my mother was about twenty feet away from me and, through three-bedroom walls, rushed to my rescue. She said heard my light moaning while visiting with my friend's mother. How that is possible? Did my guiding angel mimic my sounds to mothers' ears? You to be the judge of that.

Let's look into a Bible passage regarding my claims and belief. The Bible defiantly describes how God sends angels to protect us:

> If you say, "The Lord is my refuge," and you make the Highest your dwelling, no harm will overtake you, no disaster will come near your tent. For he will command his angels concerning you to guard you in all your ways; they will lift you up in their hands, so that you will not strike your foot against a stone. (Psalm 91:9–12)

Protection of Angels

As the above verses explain, God commands his angels to guard us in all things. It also says that when we call God our refuge and make Him our dwelling place, He is willing to keep and protect us, so that no evil can reach us. The devil tried to tempt Jesus by quoting this very verse, as stated in Matthew 4:6: "If you are the Son of God," he said, "throw yourself down. For it is written: 'He will command his angels concerning you, and they will lift you up in their hands, so that you will not strike your foot against a stone.'"

From my research, the word "angel" is, in the Old Testament, from the Hebrew word *Malak Yahwe*, which means the "God's messenger," and in the New Testament, the Greek word *angelos* also means "messenger." Therefore, angels are believed to be God's soldiers, messengers, and helpers. And there are other names for angels in the Bible, such as "sons of God," "holy ones," and "spirits."

Let's discover where the Bible depicts the duties of angels. The Bible indicates they are divided into thrones, principalities, and powers as stated in Colossians 1:16: "For by him all things were created, in heaven and on earth, visible and invisible, whether thrones or dominions or rulers or authorities-all things were created through him and for him. And, added "abilities" to angels are stated in Ephesians 1:21 "far above all rule and authority, power and dominion, and every name that is invoked, not only in the present age but also in the one to come." And when Jude 9 introduces Michael as an "archangel," it is telling us that there is a rank and order to the angel.

Two Spiritual Beings

God created two spiritual beings: angels and humans. However, there is a difference between angels and humans. The difference is that humans have a body, while angels have only a spirit. Therefore, angels are defined as created spiritual beings who have personality, that is, intellect, emotions, and will, but no body. There are more than two hundred biblical references to angels, and the first mention of angels in the Bible is in Genesis 18, where three angels in human form prophesied to Abraham that his descendants would be multiplied:

> The Lord appeared to Abraham near the great trees of Mamre while he was sitting at the entrance to his tent in the heat of the day. Abraham looked up and saw three men standing nearby. When he saw them, he hurried from the entrance of his tent to meet them and bowed low to the ground. He said, "If I have found favor in your eyes, my lord, do not pass your servant by. Let a little

water be brought, and then you may all wash your feet and rest under this tree. Let me get you something to eat, so you can be refreshed and then go on your way—now that you have come to your servant. "Very well," they answered, "do as you say."

There are also passages in the New Testament that speak of angelic manifestations appearing in human flesh as stated in Hebrews 13:1-2: "Keep on loving one another as brothers and sisters. Do not forget to show hospitality to strangers, for by so doing some people have shown hospitality to angels without knowing it." Angels are a part of God's creation, all "things visible and invisible," as stated in Colossians 1:16: "For in him all things were created: things in heaven and on earth, visible and invisible, whether thrones or powers or rulers or authorities; all things have been created through him and for him."

Given that angels belong to the realm of the invisible, it stands to reason that they, like all other aspects of creation, were brought into being by the divine Word. The Bible asserts that the entirety of existence was shaped by God's utterance, thus affirming that all domains, barring humanity, owe their existence to this divine command.

Angels, being spiritual entities, lack physical bodies, refrain from marriage, and are exempt from mortality, as stated in Matthew 22:3: "At the resurrection people will neither marry nor be given in marriage; they will be like the angels in heaven." And as stated in Luke 20:6: "and they can no longer die; for they are like the angels. They are God's children, since they are children of the resurrection." Therefore, we cannot see angels unless God specifically allows us to see them. However, angels have sometimes appeared before people in physical form. Not believing in the existence of angels because we can't see them with our naked eyes is a reason not to study the Bible properly and correctly.

Types of Angels

There are three types of angels in the Bible: cherubim, seraphim, and creatures. God rides on them as stated in Psalm 18:10: "He mounted the cherubim and flew; he soared on the wings of the wind." Visions with cherubim also describe God as seated among the cherubim. Cherubim have come to symbolize God's presence. The veil of the tabernacle was embroidered with cherubim:

> I looked, and I saw the likeness of a throne of lapis lazuli above the vault that was over the heads of the cherubim. The Lord said to the man clothed in linen, "Go in among the wheels beneath the cherubim. Fill your hands with burning coals from among the cherubim and scatter them over the city." (Ezekiel 10:1–2)

The lid of the ark of the covenant, situated within the holy of holies, featured two cherubim whose wings met in an arch. Additionally, cherubim were entrusted with the duty of safeguarding the Garden of Eden as stated in Genesis 3:24: "After he drove the man out, he placed on the east side of the Garden of Eden cherubim and a flaming sword flashing back and forth to guard the way to the tree of life." In this context, the presence of cherubim signifies God's presence in Eden. Wherever God chooses to dwell among humans, cherubim are invariably depicted. They are often portrayed with two wings covering their faces.

And the seraphim are featured in Isaiah 6:1–7, which depicted the seraphim around God's throne, engaged in ceaseless worship and adoration. They are portrayed with six wings: two covering their faces, two veiling their feet, and two in perpetual motion. Their hymn resounds with the declaration, "Holy, holy, holy, is the Lord of hosts, whose glory fills the whole earth." Their act of covering their faces and feet with their wings symbolizes reverence in the presence of God's holiness and splendor. When Isaiah, feeling unclean after encountering God, expressed his distress, it was the seraphim who purified him by applying a burning coal to his lips, cleansing him of his impurity.

> In the year that King Uzziah died, I saw the Lord, high and exalted, seated on a throne; and the train of his robe filled the temple. Above him were seraphim, each with six wings: With two wings they covered their faces, with two they covered their feet, and with two they were flying. And they were calling to one another: "Holy, holy, holy is the Lord Almighty; the whole earth is full of his glory." At the sound of their voices the doorposts and thresholds shook, and the temple was filled with smoke. "Woe to me!" I cried. "I am ruined! For I am a man of unclean lips, and I live among a people of unclean lips, and my eyes have seen the King, the Lord Almighty." Then one of the seraphim flew to me with a live coal in his hand, which he had taken with tongs from the altar. With it he touched my mouth and said, "See, this has touched your lips; your guilt is taken away and your sin atoned for." (Isaiah 6:1–7)

In both Ezekiel and Revelation, we encounter extraordinary beings surrounding the throne of God. These beings possess the visages of a lion, an ox, a human, and an eagle, perpetually offering worship to the Almighty. The symbolism of these four creatures resonates with the four facets of Jesus. He is likened to a lion, signifying His role as the ultimate King; He embodies the sacrificial nature of a bull, offering Himself to atone for human sin; His incarnation in human form reflects His mission to die on behalf of humanity; and His likeness to an eagle, the sovereign of the skies, represents His divine origin as the Son of God descended from heaven.

Angels' Protection over People

Angels possess abilities that surpass those of humans. Although they are just one category of beings, they wield powers beyond human comprehension. While humans are limited in their capabilities, angels operate with a scope of authority that lies beyond our grasp. It's acknowledged that during their earthly existence, humans were considered inferior to angels, as stated in Hebrews

2:7: "You made them a little lower than the angels; you crowned them with glory and honor."

Endowed with the authority to execute God's will, angels were referred to as powers, principalities, and dominions. During the invasion of Southern Judah by the Assyrians, Hezekiah beseeched God for deliverance, and in answer to his prayer, an angel dispatched by God swiftly decimated 185,000 soldiers of the Assyrian army in a single night: "Then the angel of the Lord went out and put to death a hundred and eighty-five thousand in the Assyrian camp. When the people got up the next morning—there were all the dead bodies!" (Isaiah 37:36).

Angels are dispatched to safeguard humans from God's will, giving rise to the notion of guardian angels. Numerous other scriptures attest to this protective role of angels. Jesus himself implores us not to disregard even the least among us, as stated in Matthew 18:10: "See that you do not despise one of these little ones. For I tell you that their angels in heaven always see the face of my Father in heaven." And here's what the angels did to defend Daniel when he was thrown into the lions' den: "My God sent his angel, and he shut the mouths of the lions. They have not hurt me, because I was found innocent in his sight. Nor have I ever done any wrong before you, Your Majesty" (Daniel 6:22). Additionally, we can find more of angels' help in Acts 12:7–11:

> Suddenly an angel of the Lord appeared, and a light shone in the cell. He struck Peter on the side and woke him up. "Quick, get up!" he said, and the chains fell off Peter's wrists. Then the angel said to him, "Put on your clothes and sandals." And Peter did so. "Wrap your cloak around you and follow me," the angel told him.
>
> Peter followed him out of the prison, but he had no idea that what the angel was doing was really happening; he thought he was seeing a vision. They passed the first and second guards and came to the iron gate leading to the city. It opened for them by itself, and they went through it. When they had walked the length of one street, suddenly the angel left him.

> Then Peter came to himself and said, "Now I know without a doubt that the Lord has sent his angel and rescued me from Herod's clutches and from everything the Jewish people were hoping would happen."

When Peter is incarcerated for spreading the gospel, an angel miraculously appears, freeing him from his chains and prison confines. Upon Peter's return to the disciples, he knocks at the door, prompting a joyful response from a woman named Rhoda, who recognizes his voice. Yet, in her excitement, she neglects to open the door and instead informs the praying disciples of Peter's presence. Despite their fervent prayers being answered, the disciples dismiss Rhoda's news as absurd until she persists, suggesting that it may be Peter's guardian angel. This skepticism mirrors our own doubts at times.

These accounts serve as poignant reminders that angels indeed watch over us. Whether they are individually assigned to provide personal protection or act in localized contexts as needed remains a mystery. However, I've never personally witnessed angels appearing before me in times of need. Yet, I've experienced an overwhelming sense of divine presence, energy, and power surrounding me during these moments.

Angels are actively safeguarding and watching over us in our daily lives. It's crucial not to lose hope or succumb to despair, regardless of the challenges we face, as angels stand ready to assist us. Each time we offer our prayers, angels play a pivotal role in conveying them to heaven. Instead of yielding to discouragement, we should turn to prayer. Moreover, it's imperative that we refrain from belittling, ignoring, gossiping about, or causing hardship to others. This is because each individual is under the guardianship of an angel who gazes upon the face of God daily.

How does it feel to acknowledge that there are unseen angels all around us who are watching over us and protecting us? Do you believe in angels now?

Chapter 11

Prayer

Christian Prayer

IN CHRISTIANITY, PRAYER HOLDS a central place, emphasizing a deep connection with the Divine. Those who engage in frequent prayer are often seen as spiritually attuned, drawing closer to the divine presence.

What it means by call on God in prayer?

To calling on God is not merely to raise one's voice, but to invoke the divine presence with a heartfelt and spiritual intensity, uttering the sacred "Abba, Father" with profound love. It's the genuine expression of truth and power emanating from the depths of the soul, a lamentation that unites body and spirit in a singular purpose. It's the mingling of tears and sweat, a fervent outpouring of love and prayer from the depths of the heart.

God knows everything, so why shouldn't we pray?

In God's creation of humanity, He bestowed upon us not only eyes to see and a nose to smell but also a mouth—the gateway through which communication flows from us. Our thoughts are processed by our brains, and the words we wish to express are articulated by our mouths. Whether spoken from the depths of sincerity or cloaked in embellishment, the words that escape our lips carry immense power.

Prayer is not transmitting mere requests for material possessions or a comfortable life or a wish list. Instead, it serves as a conduit for forging a deeper connection with God and aligning ourselves with His divine purpose. It involves not only seeking His guidance but also obeying His commands, which are reiterated throughout His Word. Thus, the essence of prayer lies not in self-centered desires but in surrendering to God's will, recognizing that our ultimate purpose is to glorify Him.

Did He not affirm that everything you earnestly ask for in prayer will be granted to you, provided you harbor no doubts? For such unwavering trust constitutes true faith—believing in the promises of God's Word. The Bible reassures us that God rewards those who diligently seek Him, and He bestows blessings upon those who approach Him in faith-filled prayer:

> Now faith is confidence in what we hope for and assurance about what we do not see. This is what the ancients were commended for. By faith we understand that the universe was formed at God's command, so that what is seen was not made out of what was visible. By faith Abel brought God a better offering than Cain did. By faith he was commended as righteous, when God spoke well of his offerings. And by faith Abel still speaks, even though he is dead. By faith Enoch was taken from this life, so that he did not experience death: "He could not be found, because God had taken him away." For before he was taken, he was commended as one who pleased God. And without faith it is impossible to please God, because anyone who comes to him must believe that he exists and that he rewards those who earnestly seek him. (Hebrews 11:1-6)

Bible Verses about Prayer

Rejoice always, pray continually, give thanks in all circumstances; for this is God's will for you in Christ Jesus. (1 Thessalonians 5:16-18)

"Ask and it will be given to you; seek and you will find; knock and the door will be opened to you. For everyone who asks receives; the one who seeks finds; and to the one who knocks, the door will be opened." (Matthew 7:7-8)

"Therefore I tell you, whatever you ask for in prayer, believe that you have received it, and it will be your" (Mark 11:21)

Do not be anxious about anything, but in every situation, by prayer and petition, with thanksgiving, present your requests to God. And the peace of God, which transcends all understanding, will guard your hearts and your minds in Christ Jesus. (Philippians 4:6-7)

"Then you will call on me and come and pray to me, and I will listen to you." (Jeremiah 29:12)

This is what the Lord says, he who made the earth, the Lord who formed it and established it—the Lord is his name: 'Call to me and I will answer you and tell you great and unsearchable things you do not know.' (Jeremiah 33:2-3)

"As for me, far be it from me that I should sin against the Lord by failing to pray for you. And I will teach you the way that is good and right." (1 Samuel 12:23)

"If my people, which are called by my name, shall humble themselves, and pray, and seek my face, and turn from their wicked ways; then will I hear from heaven, and will forgive their sin, and will heal their land." (2 Chronicles 7:14)

The Lord is near to all who call on him, to all who call on him in truth. (Psalm 145:18)

The Lord detests the sacrifice of the wicked, but the prayer of the upright pleases him. (Proverbs 15:8)

The Lord is far from the wicked, but he hears the prayer of the righteous. (Proverbs 15:29)

"But when you pray, go into your room, close the door and pray to your Father, who is unseen. Then your Father, who sees what is done in secret, will reward you. And when you pray, do not keep on babbling like pagans, for they think they will be heard because of their many words." (Matthew 6:6–7)

"Again, truly I tell you that if two of you on earth agree about anything they ask for, it will be done for them by my Father in heaven. For where two or three gather in my name, there am I with them." (Matthew 18:19–20)

"If you believe, you will receive whatever you ask for in prayer." (Matthew 21:22)

"Watch and pray so that you will not fall into temptation. The spirit is willing, but the flesh is weak." (Matthew 26:41)

He said to them, "When you pray, say: 'Father, hallowed be your name, your kingdom come.'" (Luke 11:2)

In the same way, the Spirit helps us in our weakness. We do not know what we ought to pray for, but the Spirit himself intercedes for us through wordless groans. (Romans 8:26)

Devote yourselves to prayer, being watchful and thankful. (Colossians 4:2)

If any of you lacks wisdom, let him ask of God, who gives to all liberally and without reproach, and it will be given to him. But let him ask in faith, with no doubting, for he who doubts is like a wave of the sea driven and tossed by the wind. For let not that man suppose that he will receive anything from the Lord. (James 1:5–7)

Therefore, confess your sins to each other and pray for each other so that you may be healed. The prayer of a righteous person is powerful and effective. (James 5:16)

> This is the confidence we have in approaching God: that if we ask anything according to his will, he hears us. And if we know that he hears us—whatever we ask—we know that we have what we asked of him. (1 John 5:14-15)

Summary of Above Verses

The essence of prayer and faith is encapsulated in the parables of asking, seeking, and knocking, which promise that those who approach God with unwavering faith will receive, find, and have doors opened to them. These teachings underscore the importance of persistent prayer and steadfast faith.

In our prayer life, it's crucial to approach God with unwavering faith, avoiding doubt and aimless repetition. Rather, we're encouraged to retreat to a quiet place, shut out distractions, and commune with our Father in heaven. We're reminded not to mimic the frantic prayers of the Gentiles, who believe that their verbosity earns them favor with God.

Furthermore, practicing the power of prayer entails interceding for one another and confessing our sins, fostering a sense of community and deepening our connection with God. Ultimately, the message emphasizes the importance of believing that our prayers align with God's will and living our lives accordingly. It's a call to combine faith-filled prayer with tangible action, completing the journey of faith.

A Spiritual Key

Prayer is not just saying words to God. It's a spiritual key to unlock God's abundant treasure for each of us and for our hearts and minds to receive God's blessing. Each word conveys a plea drenched in faith and hope, especially channeling God's grace for the meaningful days to come. Make a commitment to prayer daily or think about it, no matter where you are—at home or in your car during your commute to work, or going anywhere to your own directions, or in moments when you are alone in peace and quiet.

When you consciously choose to immerse yourself in God's love and embrace His promises, walking under His guidance, you open yourself to experiencing His mighty hand of deliverance and hope. It's a profound realization that you're not journeying alone, but rather you're guided, guarded, and blessed by the almighty God. This underscores the potency of unwavering prayer, anchored in faith and conviction.

Let us fully embrace the power of prayer, allowing every word to resonate deeply within us, fortifying our faith and nurturing our spirit. Embrace the abundant blessings that God has prepared for us, and trust in His protective embrace. Through prayer, we can experience deliverance from anything that seeks to hold us back or weigh us down. Just as nature undergoes renewal and growth, so too can our souls experience rejuvenation and transformation. Let us embrace this season of new beginnings, allowing our spirits to blossom with fresh possibilities in our spiritual journey.

Every day, amidst the splendor of creation, we serve a God whose nature is unchanging, yesterday, today, and forever. Even when the world we live in is filled with anxiety and nervousness, and the days ahead are filled with uncertainty, God stands as our unwavering and steadfast rock. Anchored in our faith, we eagerly anticipate witnessing the miraculous hand of God at work in our lives. Gracious and merciful heavenly Father, Lord God almighty, you are the Alpha and the Omega, the King of kings and Lord of lords. You are the origin and the culmination, the primal and the ultimate.

Daily Prayer

Heavenly Father, as we awaken to a new day, we lift our hearts in prayer. Guide us as we embark on the day's journey, shielding us from the influence of evil that may seek to disrupt our path, interactions, and endeavors. May our actions and words reflect Your presence within us, illuminating our relationships and shining as a beacon of Your light to the world. Grant us the strength to be the preserving salt that enhances the flavor of life, rather than salt that has lost its savor. I am deeply grateful for the opportunity to extend help and support to numerous individuals, providing them with blessings of health, safety, and financial stability.

In the midst of life's many trials, we turn to You for solace and strength. As the world cries out in anguish, we lift our voices in prayer to You in the quite room from the bottom of our heart. Illuminate the path of Your children, granting them victory over adversity. Remember those weighed down by weariness, illness, and poverty. Take them gently by the mighty hand, that they may find endurance and joy in their tribulations. We implore Your remembrance, for all humanity depends on Your mercy. Send forth Your Holy Spirit to aid us on our journey in the power of our Savior's imminent arrival, renewing our spirits and sustaining us through every trial.

Protect us now and in the days to come, as You have shielded us in times past. We lift our voices in praise, recounting the countless blessings You have bestowed upon us. May we recognize Your hand in all aspects of our lives and worship You wholeheartedly. You never forsake those who place their trust in You, nor those who love You faithfully. Remain by our side always, watching over us with Your loving gaze. Grant us the courage and fortitude to serve You diligently each day, wherever life may lead us. May our actions reflect Your love and grace, drawing others to You through our witness.

I lift up my family and friends in prayer, asking for Your abundant blessings to encompass each of them. May Your hand of protection guard them, your healing touch sustain their health, and Your provision supply their needs abundantly. Shower them with an avalanche of blessings in all aspects of their lives, granting them prosperity, joy, and fulfillment. Endow them with wisdom to navigate life's challenges, and may Your guiding presence illuminate their paths.

Dear Lord, with the deepest sincerity of my soul, I invoke the holy name of my Savior and Lord, Jesus Christ, and present to you my most heartfelt prayer. May you guide my path, shield me from harm, and mold me in the likeness of Enoch, who walked faithfully with you, always striving to please. Though I am but an ordinary soul, you have graciously singled me out to lead, protect, and accompany me on this journey of life. I trust in your divine knowledge of my needs, unseen to my own eyes, and believe that you will be by my side until the end, clasping my hand with your loving grip. Your boundless love fills me with warmth and reassurance whenever I lift my voice in prayer, infusing my heart with hope and gratitude. In the name of our Lord Jesus, I offer this prayer. Amen.

www.ingramcontent.com/pod-product-compliance
Lightning Source LLC
Chambersburg PA
CBHW060412090426
42734CB00011B/2294